STATISTICS OF EDUCATION

Teachers in England

2001 *Edition*

(including teachers pay for England and Wales)

London: The Stationery Office

ISBN 0 11 271127 8

Contents

Introduction

This edition of "Statistics of Education: Teachers in England 2001 edition(including teachers pay for England and Wales)" provides updated information on the teaching force, generally to March 2000.

Tables have been grouped into sections for ease of use. The team responsible for producing the volume were : Andrew Clarke, Isabella Craig, Dean Franklin, Tom Lind-Jackson and John Pascoe.

Explanatory Notes and Definitions

Sources and coverage

1 The statistics in this volume are derived from a number of sources:

Table number(s)	Source
1	TTA ITT Trainee Numbers Census
3-13, 21, 22-26, 32-40, 48-51b, 53-58	Database of Teacher Records (DTR)
14, 16-20, 31, 41-45, 52	DfEE and National Assembly for Wales 618g surveys
15, 27-30	1996/97 Secondary Schools Curriculum & Staffing Survey (SSCSS)
46-50, 55, 58	Pensioner Statistical System (PENSTATS)

2 The Database of Teacher' Records (DTR) is the Department's main source of teachers' service and salary records and provides information as at 31 March of the year in question. All DTR data for March 1998, 1999 and 2000 are provisional. The tables compiled from the 618G survey, a return of teachers numbers and vacant posts made by local education authorities, show the position as at January of each year shown. The SSCSS is a sample survey of maintained secondary schools in England conducted by DfES in November 1996.

Initial teacher training

3 In order to teach in a maintained school, teachers are normally required to have qualified teacher status (QTS). This is usually obtained by successfully completing a course of initial teacher training (ITT) at an accredited institution whose provision meets the Secretary of State's criteria for ITT. Two popular routes to achieving qualified teacher status in England and Wales are: by successful completion of an undergraduate course of initial teacher training or of a course leading to the postgraduate certificate in education (PGCE). Both types of courses are run by higher education institutions. In 1993 a new system of school centred ITT (SCITT) was launched. This is postgraduate training that is designed and delivered by groups of schools. The graduate teacher programme and registered teacher programme came into force on 1 December 1997, replacing the licensed teacher scheme. Table 7a(iv) and 7b(iv) shows those individuals entering teaching through these routes.

Teacher flows

4 In tables showing teachers entering and leaving service in the maintained schools sector, teachers moving between full-time and part-time service are not counted as entrants or leavers.

Teachers in service in LEA schools (including formerly grant maintained schools)

5 The tables cover LEA maintained schools (including formerly grant maintained schools). Under the 1988 Education Reform Act, all LEA schools, with the exception of nursery schools, could apply for grant-maintained status. Prior to September 1999, grant-maintained schools received their funding from the government via the Funding Agency for Schools. The first schools were given self-governing status from Autumn 1989. Legislation introduced in September 1999 meant that grant maintained schools would become part of the LEA maintained sector. The separate types of school shown in some tables are explained below.

a Nursery schools provide education primarily for children below compulsory school age, i.e. under 5.

b Primary schools consist mainly of infant schools for children aged 5 to 7, junior schools for those aged 7 to 11 and junior and infant schools for both age groups. Some areas have first schools that cater for ages from 5 to 8, 9 or 10: these are the first stage of a three-tier (first, middle and secondary) school system. Many primary schools provide nursery classes for children under 5. A nursery class is one so designated by the local education authority.

c Middle schools take children from first schools and generally feed comprehensive upper schools. They cater for older junior and younger senior pupils. They cover varying age ranges e.g. 8 to 12, 9 to 12, 9 to 13, 10 to 13 and 10 to 14. Those for pupils aged 8 to 12 and 9 to 12 are deemed primary, those for ages 10 to 13 and 10 to 14 are deemed secondary and those for ages 9 to 13 may be deemed either primary or secondary. Where middle schools are not separated they are shown as primary or secondary as appropriate.

d There are three main types of secondary schools: modern, grammar and comprehensive. From 1 April 1993, sixth form colleges were reclassified as part of the further education sector and are thus excluded from secondary schools from that date onwards.

6 Teachers who divide their service between primary and secondary schools are shown as 'divided service'. The 'miscellaneous' group includes, for example, those in camp schools and in centres for English as an additional language.

7 Tables relating to maintained nursery, primary and secondary schools cover teachers who hold qualified teacher status and licensed teachers working towards it and include all or some of the following categories.

a Trained teachers.

b Graduate and graduate equivalent teachers (i.e. those with a university degree or qualification which is recognised for the purposes of payment of the graduate addition to salaries), who are untrained and whose graduation or obtaining of a graduate equivalent qualification either preceded the introduction of a training requirement for graduates or equivalents or who are otherwise exempt from that requirement.

c   Teachers with certain specialist qualifications (e.g. in art and music).

d   Teachers who were granted qualified teacher status either on the basis of service as uncertificated teachers (or equivalent) prior to 1 April 1945 or under the Schools (Amendment) Regulations 1968.

e   Teachers who have undertaken approved teacher training, or obtained approved qualifications outside the United Kingdom.

f   Trained teachers who are nationals of a member state of the EC, and are recognised and permitted to teach in that, or another, member state of the EC.

g   Teachers who were previously employed as licensed teachers, under the terms of the Education (Teachers) Regulations 1989, and have been informed, on behalf of the Secretary of State, that they are recognised as qualified teachers for teaching in schools in England and Wales.

8   The only categories of unqualified teacher which can be appointed to maintained primary and secondary schools are as follows.

a   Students on teaching practice (formerly temporary assistant teachers) - mainly candidates awaiting entry to courses of initial teacher training in establishments of further education.

b   Instructors - teachers not employed in a general capacity, but who possess specialist knowledge of a particular art or skill (e.g. music, sport) who are employed only where qualified teachers of that art or skill are not available.

c   Teachers on the graduate teacher / licensed teachers scheme and registered teaching programme / overseas trained teachers scheme.

9   Teachers in occasional service, i.e. teachers engaged on a short term basis, are included only in analyses derived from Form 618G.

Special schools

10. Special schools, either day or boarding, provide education for children with special educational needs who cannot be educated satisfactorily in an ordinary school. Maintained special schools are run by local education authorities who pay all the expenses of maintenance.

11   Non-maintained special schools are run by voluntary bodies; they may apply for a grant from the Department for Education and Employment for capital work and for equipment but their current expenditure is met primarily from the fees charged to the local education authorities for pupils sent to the schools.

12   For tables 27-30 the subjects were grouped according to the following classification:

Subject	Includes (for example)
Mathematics	Pure Maths, Applied Maths, Statistics
English	English Literature
Biology	Human Biology, Botany, Zoology
Chemistry	
Physics	
Combined/General Sciences	Integrated Science, Double Award Science, Single Award Science
Other Sciences	Geology, Environmental Science, Rural Science, Agricultural Science, Science in Society
French	
German	
Spanish	
Other Modern Languages	Italian, Russian, Modern Greek, Modern Hebrew, Asian Languages, Welsh
Design and Technology	Design and Realisation, Graphics, Graphic Communication, Craft, Metalwork, Woodwork, Food Technology
Information Technology	Computer Studies
Other Technology	For classes taken by pupils-Combined Technology (i.e. lessons covering both D&T and IT);for teachers' qualifications-other technology subjects (e.g. Engineering)
Home Economics	Food and Nutrition, Dress, Textiles, Child Development
Business Studies	
Classics	Ancient Greek, Latin, Classical Civilisation, Ancient
Hebrew	
History	
Religious Education	
Geography	
Other Social Studies	Economics, Sociology, Physiology, Area Studies, Archaeology, Law, Philosophy, Politics
Combined Arts/Humanities/Social Studies	Modular Humanities, Integrated Humanities
Music	History of Music
Drama	Media Studies, Communication Studies, Expressive Arts
Art	Art and Design, Creative Arts, Pottery, Jewellery, History of Art
Physical Education	Dance, Outdoor Education
Careers Education	
Personal and Social Education	Health Education, Preparation for Adult Life, Work Experience
General Studies	
General Primary Subjects	
Other	SEN, Vocational Studies

13   The staffing of special schools comprises qualified teachers, student teachers, instructors and certain other unqualified teachers. The latter group are mainly teachers of children with Special Educational Needs who were transferred to the education service on 1 April 1971, having previously been employed by local health

authorities. They are not included in any of the tables in this volume. Some of them will eventually become qualified teachers after serving for a prescribed period in a special school.

Direct grant schools
14 From October 1980 these schools, with the exception of three nursery schools, (one of which has subsequently closed), were re-classified as independent schools.

Teachers pay
15 From 1 September 1993, the Government introduced a new common 18 point pay spine for classroom teachers. A teacher's position on the new spine is determined by the total number of points awarded. A relevant body, that is, in the case of a school with a delegated budget, the school's governing body, may award points under six headings; qualifications, experience, special educational needs, recruitment and retention, responsibilities and excellence. From 1 September 1996, half spine points were introduced to the classroom teachers pay spine. More detailed information on teachers pay scales can be found in the School Teachers Pay and Conditions Document, published annually by this Department.

16 Head teachers and deputy head teachers have a separate pay system with 51 incremental points. A head or deputy head teachers pay is determined by a number of factors including: responsibilities of the post; social, economic and cultural background of the pupils attending; and the group number to which the school is assigned.

Promotions
17 Table 40 shows the numbers of teachers whose grading on the DTR has been changed either from classroom teacher to head teacheror from deputy head to head teacher.

Vacancies
18 The vacancies information is taken from the Form 618g survey. The number of vacancies are counted on the survey date, which is the third Thursday in January of each year. Local education authorities are asked only to count those vacancies for posts which are full-time, permanent and advertised on the survey date.

Retirements
19 Retirement benefits can be awarded on age ground, if upon reaching age 60, on premature ground, an employer makes a teacher redundant, whether on efficiency or other grounds, or infirmity grounds, where a teacher is aged under 60 and has to retire on ill-health grounds. All retirement data is for the year in which a pension was first paid, not the year of the last day of service, for example if a person retires on 31 March their

pension will be paid in April for the first time so they are counted in a different financial year to the year in which they left work.

Further and higher education
20 Where statistics on the further and higher education sector are provided these comprise all full-time teachers in adult education centres, youth welfare centres, and nursery training centres, as well as higher and further education establishments outside the 'old' university sector. Not all higher education academic staff are shown, because they are not all members of the Teachers Pension Scheme and therefore are not included on the DTR. Figures for 1993-94 onwards include sixth form colleges. The data for 1998, 1999 and 2000 are provisional. A description of the main establishments covered is as follows.

a Former polytechnics and HE colleges now funded by the HE Funding Councils and FE colleges funded by the FE Funding Council.

b Adult education centres. These are establishments maintained by local education authorities which provide a wide range of courses, many of them of a recreational type, mainly for evening students. These centres were formerly given the title "evening institutes". The majority of the staff of adult education centres are employed part-time. Only full-time teachers are included in DTR statistics.

21 No figures are included for teachers in university departments of education, university art teaching training centres and other university departments.

22 Not all graduate teachers in further and higher education are recorded as such and some therefore appear as non-graduates in the tables. Teachers whose degree entitles them to a salary addition are not affected.

Degree subjects
23 For comparability with earlier volumes, in most tables where subjects are shown, graduate teachers have been analysed under the standardised subject groups of the pre 1987 United Kingdom Subject Classification for Education Statistics. However, where the heading "mathematics" is separately shown it consists of those holding degrees in mathematics only together with those with degrees in mathematics and physics in combination; other combinations of mathematics with science appear under 'other science'. Tables 24a and 24b, however, show the number of graduate teachers in nursery, primary and secondary schools who hold degrees in particular subjects. The subjects of the degree have each been allocated to one of 10 subject headings.

Regional analysis
24 The regions shown in the tables include the local education authorities shown below. Since 1 April 1996, a series of local government reorganisations have taken

place in England and Wales. The effects of these changes impact on this edition of the volume.

North East:
Gateshead, Newcastle-upon-Tyne, North Tyneside, South Tyneside, Sunderland, Hartlepool, Middlesbrough, Redcar & Cleveland, Stockton-on-Tees, Darlington, Durham, Northumberland.

North West:
Cumbria, Cheshire, Halton, Warrington, Bolton, Bury, Manchester, Oldham, Rochdale, Salford, Stockport, Tameside, Trafford, Wigan, Lancashire, Blackburn with Darwen, Blackpool, Knowsley, Liverpool, St Helens, Sefton, Wirral.

Yorkshire and The Humber:
City of Kingston-upon-Hull, East Riding of Yorkshire, North East Lincolnshire, North Lincolnshire, North Yorkshire, York, Barnsley, Doncaster, Rotherham, Sheffield, Bradford, Calderdale, Kirklees, Leeds, Wakefield.

East Midlands:
Derbyshire, Derby, Leicestershire, Leicester City, Rutland, Lincolnshire, Northamptonshire, Nottinghamshire, City of Nottingham.

West Midlands:
Herefordshire, Worcestershire, Shropshire, Telford and Wrekin, Staffordshire, Stoke, Warwickshire, Birmingham, Coventry, Dudley, Sandwell, Solihull, Walsall, Wolverhampton.

East of England:
Cambridgeshire, City of Peterborough, Norfolk, Suffolk, Bedfordshire, Luton, Essex, Southend, Thurrock, Hertfordshire.

London:
Barking and Dagenham, Barnet, Bexley, Brent, Bromley, Camden, City of London, Croydon, Ealing, Enfield, Greenwich, Hackney, Hammersmith & Fulham, Haringey, Harrow, Havering, Hillingdon, Hounslow, Islington, Kensington & Chelsea, Kingston-upon-Thames, Lambeth, Lewisham, Merton, Newham, Redbridge, Richmond-upon- Thames, Southwark, Sutton, Tower Hamlets, Waltham Forest, Wandsworth, Westminster.

South East:
Bracknell Forest, Windsor and Maidenhead, West Berkshire, Reading, Slough, Wokingham, Buckinghamshire, Milton Keynes, East Sussex, Brighton and Hove, Hampshire, Portsmouth, Southampton, Isle of Wight, Kent, Medway, Oxfordshire, Surrey, West Sussex.

South West:
Isles of Scilly, Bath & NE Somerset, City of Bristol, North Somerset, South Gloucestershire, Cornwall, Devon, City of Plymouth, Torbay, Dorset, Poole, Bournemouth, Gloucestershire, Somerset, Wiltshire, Swindon.

Wales:
Anglesey, Gwynedd, Conwy, Denbighshire, Flintshire, Wrexham, Powys, Ceredigion, Pembrokeshire, Carmarthenshire, Swansea, Neath & Port Talbot, Bridgend, Vale of Glamorgan, Rhondda CT, Merthyr Tydfil, Caerphilly, Blaenau Gwent, Torfaen, Monmouthshire, Newport, Cardiff.

Changes in coverage
The coverage of many of the tables has changed slightly from previous editions. Many of the tables which use data from the DTR previously covered teachers in maintained nursery, primary and secondary schools, but now cover all teachers in the maintained schools sector (i.e. including special schools and pupil referral units.) Similarly, many of these tables previously included small numbers of teachers without Qualified Teacher Status (QTS), but are now qualified only.

Symbols used

.   not applicable

..   not available

-    nil or negligible

INITIAL TEACHER TRAINING
Recruitment to initial teacher training courses[1]: academic years 1997/98 to 2001/02 by sector and subject specialism

ENGLAND

	1997/98	1998/99	1999/00	2000/01	2001/02			Percentage increase 2000/01 to 2001/02
					Actual	Target	% diff. +/-	
Primary and secondary								
Undergraduate	9,620	8,790	8,510	8,100	7,830	-	-	-3
Postgraduate	18,100	17,420	17,460	19,620	21,180	-	-	8
Of which								
School centred/ other non-HEI	670	770	830	1,060	1,190	-	-	12
Total	27,720	26,210	25,970	27,720	29,000	29,890	-3	5
Primary								
Undergraduate	7,070	6,710	6,640	6,580	6,380	-	-	-3
Postgraduate	4,680	5,120	5,450	6,590	6,670	-	-	1
Of which								
School centred/ other non-HEI	210	370	430	510	590	-	-	15
Total	11,750	11,830	12,100	13,170	13,060	12,500	4	-1
Secondary								
Undergraduate	2,540	2,090	1,860	1,520	1,440	-	-	-5
Postgraduate	13,420	12,290	12,010	13,020	14,510	-	-	11
Of which								
School centred/ other non-HEI	460	410	400	550	600	-	-	9
Total	15,970	14,380	13,870	14,540	15,950	17,390	-8	10
Secondary by subject								
Mathematics	1,460	1,120	1,300	1,290	1,550	1,940	-20	20
English (inc. Drama)	2,140	2,130	2,030	2,030	2,230	2,160	3	10
Science	2,790	2,280	2,360	2,410	2,590	2,810	-8	7
Modern foreign languages	1,800	1,660	1,470	1,640	1,690	2,050	-17	3
Technology[2]	1,980	1,680	1,700	1,860	2,140	2,150	0	15
History	960	900	820	910	920	900	2	1
Geography	850	750	870	900	1,030	1,175	-13	14
Physical education	1,640	1,490	1,190	1,210	1,330	1,200	11	10
Art	900	900	800	850	840	850	-1	-1
Music	500	490	520	560	650	705	-8	16
Religious education	640	620	530	570	590	650	-10	3
Other[3]	300	360	280	320	390	450	-13	23
Margin of flexibility[4]	n/a	n/a	n/a	n/a	n/a	350		
Total	15,970	14,380	13,870	14,540	15,950	17,390	-8	10

Sources: TTA's ITT Trainee Numbers Census 1997/98 - 2001/02
Targets - DfES

1. Recruitment figures for 2001/02 are provisional and are subject to change.
2. Includes Universities and other HE institutions, SCITT and OU. Recruitment numbers shown are rounded to the nearest 10. Percentages have been calculated on the actual figure, rather than the rounded."
3. Technology includes design and technology, information technology, business studies and home economics.
4. Other includes citizenship, classics, economics, social studies, and other subjects.
5. 2001/02 was the first year of recruitment for citizenship.
6. The margin of flexibility included in the England targets from 2000/01 is equivalent to the provision the Teacher Training
7. Agency had in 1999/2000 to "vire" places between secondary subjects within certain parameters, but is now given explicitly.

2 INITIAL TEACHER TRAINING
Initial teacher training intake targets: Academic year 2002/03

ENGLAND

	2002/03
Primary	14,000
Secondary	17,790
Of which:	
Mathematics	1,940
English	2,100
Drama	250
Science	2,850
Modern foreign languages	2,050
Technology[1]	2,500
History	950
Geography	1,100
PE	1,200
Art	850
Music	700
RE	700
Citizenship	200
Economics, Social Sciences, Classics, Other subjects	300
Secondary reserve[2]	100
Primary and secondary	31,790

Source: DfES

1. Technology includes design and technology, information and communications technology, and business studies.
2. The "secondary reserve" included in the targets as of 2002/03 are places that the TTA can allocate to any secondary subject, to support providers whose baseline would otherwise be below economic levels; to ensure the appropriate denominational balance; and to help providers who offer a high proportion of places in shortage subjects and who therefore have particular uncertainty of income.

3

INITIAL TEACHER TRAINING
Successful completers: calendar years 1991 to 2000 by type of course and class of degree[1,2]

ENGLAND (percentages)

	1991	1992	1993	1994	1995	1996	1997	1998[3]	1999[3]	2000[3]
PGCE										
Class of first degree										
1st honours	2.9	3.1	3.7	3.8	4.3	4.4	5.0	5.0	5.3	5.6
2nd honours	80.1	80.6	81.6	83.1	83.2	83.2	85.4	85.3	85.8	86.1
other and unclassified honours	7.2	7.8	7.4	7.1	7.0	6.0	5.2	4.7	3.9	4.1
ordinary/pass	9.8	8.5	7.3	6.1	5.5	6.5	4.4	5.0	5.0	4.3
Total	100	100	100	100	100	100	100	100	100	100
BEds										
Class of first degree										
1st honours	4.6	3.9	4.2	3.8	3.9	4.0	4.5	4.8	5.3	6.1
2nd honours	82.9	82.9	80.5	80.5	84.1	85.8	90.1	88.2	87.8	90.0
other and unclassified honours	4.5	4.4	3.2	3.4	3.1	3.0	4.0	2.8	3.5	2.9
ordinary/pass	8.0	8.9	12.1	12.4	8.9	7.3	1.4	4.2	3.4	1.0
Total	100	100	100	100	100	100	100	100	100	100

Source: Database of Teacher Records.

1. Excludes those for whom no class of degree is shown in the teachers' record system. These are mainly holders of acceptable graduate equivalent qualifications or non-UK degrees.
2. Excludes Open University and School Centered Initial Teacher Training.
3. Provisional data

INITIAL TEACHER TRAINING

4

2000 PGCE Completers: Delay between award of first degree and completion of a one-year PGCE by sex and age[1]

ENGLAND[2]

				Number of years delay				
	up to 2	between 2 and 3	between 3 and 4	between 4 and 5	between 5 and 6	between 6 and 7	7 or more	Total
Men								
under 25	910	450	190	50	-	-	-	1,600
25 to 29	150	140	190	260	210	160	180	1,280
30 to 34	90	50	40	40	40	30	290	570
35 to 39	70	40	20	10	10	10	180	340
40 to 44	40	30	10	10	-	10	120	220
45 to 49	10	10	-	0	-	-	50	90
50 to 54	-	10	-	-	-	-	30	50
55 to 59	-	-	-	-	-	-	10	10
60 & over	-	-	-	-	-	-	-	-
Total	1,280	720	460	370	260	210	870	4,170
Women								
under 25	3,210	1,420	590	130	10	-	-	5,360
25 to 29	290	260	430	520	440	310	280	2,540
30 to 34	170	100	60	40	40	40	480	920
35 to 39	160	120	50	30	20	20	430	820
40 to 44	140	100	40	20	10	10	280	600
45 to 49	40	40	20	10	10	-	110	220
50 to 54	10	10	-	-	-	-	10	30
55 to 59	-	-	-	-	-	-	-	-
60 & over	-	-	-	-	-	-	-	-
Total	4,030	2,040	1,180	750	540	390	1,590	10,500
Men and Women								
under 25	4,130	1,870	770	180	10	-	-	6,970
25 to 29	440	390	610	780	650	470	470	3,810
30 to 34	260	150	90	80	80	70	770	1,500
35 to 39	230	150	70	40	30	30	610	1,160
40 to 44	180	120	50	30	20	20	400	820
45 to 49	50	50	20	10	20	10	160	310
50 to 54	10	20	10	10	-	-	40	80
55 to 59	-	-	-	-	-	-	10	10
60 & over	-	-	-	-	-	-	-	-
Total	5,300	2,760	1,630	1,120	800	590	2,460	14,670

Source: Database of Teacher Records.

1. 2000 data are provisional.
2. Includes those trained through the Open University.

5 INITIAL TEACHER TRAINING
Successful completers: Qualification by phase of training

ENGLAND[1]

	1997			1998			1999			2000		
	BEd	PGCE	Total	BEd	PGCE	Total	BEd	PGCE	Total	BEd	PGCE	Total
Primary and secondary	9,710	16,440	26,150	8,910	15,890	24,800	8,890	15,240	24,130	6,910	14,830	21,740
Primary	7,560	4,710	12,270	7,160	4,410	11,560	7,290	4,800	12,090	5,570	4,750	10,320
Secondary	2,150	11,730	13,880	1,760	11,480	13,240	1,600	10,440	12,040	1,330	10,080	11,410
Of which:												
Mathematics	250	1,130	1,380	190	920	1,110	130	750	880	110	860	960
English (inc. Drama)	20	1,930	1,950	60	2,070	2,130	60	1,960	2,020	60	1,860	1,920
Science	220	2,100	2,320	160	1,920	2,080	140	1,640	1,780	70	1,710	1,780
Modern foreign languages	50	1,450	1,510	60	1,460	1,510	40	1,370	1,410	30	1,230	1,260
Technology	670	820	1,490	520	760	1,280	450	670	1,120	350	670	1,010
History	10	870	870	10	890	890	0	790	790	0	760	760
Geography	10	770	780	20	760	780	20	660	680	10	740	740
Art	0	840	840	0	810	810	0	800	810	10	700	710
Music	30	430	460	20	410	430	30	400	440	10	430	440
Religious education	20	510	530	30	500	530	30	500	520	20	430	450
Physical education	830	570	1,400	670	720	1,390	690	650	1,340	670	490	1,160
Other	40	320	360	20	280	300	20	240	260	10	210	220

Source: Database of Teacher Records.

1. Includes those trained through the Open University.

6 NEW ENTRANTS TO TEACHING
Successful completers calendar year 1999: sector of service in March 2000 by region of ITT

ENGLAND AND WALES[1]

	Total completers in 1999	Not in service in England and Wales 31.3.00[2,3]	In full or part-time service on 31 March 2000[3]						
			England					Wales	
			Maintained nursery and primary	Maintained secondary	Maintained special and PRU	Total maintained schools	FE, HE and Independent schools	Maintained schools sector	FE, HE and Independent schools
Government Office region of ITT									
North East	1,190	320	350	460	20	830	40	-	-
North West	3,630	930	1,210	1,340	20	2,560	100	30	-
Yorkshire and The Humber	2,820	710	910	1,110	10	2,030	70	10	-
East Midlands	1,860	400	840	550	10	1,400	60	10	-
West Midlands	2,180	520	820	750	20	1,580	80	10	-
East of England	2,020	390	800	690	10	1,510	120	-	-
London	3,940	1,100	1,460	1,240	20	2,720	120	-	-
South East	3,120	670	1,340	990	10	2,350	110	10	-
South West	2,580	660	870	900	10	1,790	100	40	-
Open University and SCITT	790	260	180	250	-	430	80	20	-
England[1]	24,130	5,940	8,780	8,290	110	17,190	870	120	10
Wales	2,480	1,060	370	210	-	580	50	770	20

Source: Database of Teacher Records.

1. Includes those trained through the Open University.
2. Some in service teachers may be shown as not in service because their service details are not recorded. These may include;
   entrants to the 'old' university sector, entrants to the independent sector who are not in the Teachers Pension Scheme (TPS), entrants to part-time service outside the maintained nursery, primary and secondary sector who are not in the TPS.
3. Provisional data. The numbers shown as in service may increase as a result of late receipt of annual service returns.

7(i) NEW ENTRANTS TO TEACHING
BEd completers: Calendar year 1999: type of service and sector by sex and age

ENGLAND[1]

	Total BEd completers England in 1999	Not in service in England 31.3.00[2,3]	In full or part-time service in England on 31 March 2000[3]				
			Maintained nursery and primary	Maintained secondary	Maintained special and PRU	Total maintained schools	FE, HE and independent schools
Men							
Under 25	810	250	310	230	-	540	20
25 to 29	310	90	90	120	-	210	10
30 to 34	200	70	50	60	10	120	10
35 to 39	150	40	40	60	-	100	10
40 to 44	90	30	20	40	-	60	-
45 to 49	50	10	10	20	-	30	-
50 to 54	10	10	-	10	-	10	-
55 & over	-	-	-	-	-	-	-
Total 1,610		490	540	530	10	1,080	50
Women							
Under 25	4,690	1,070	3,120	390	20	3,530	90
25 to 29	1,020	250	640	120	10	760	10
30 to 34	490	130	300	40	10	350	10
35 to 39	560	130	360	60	-	420	10
40 to 44	370	90	240	30	-	280	10
45 to 49	110	20	70	20	-	90	-
50 to 54	30	10	20	-	-	20	-
55 & over	-	-	-	-	-	-	-
Total 7,280		1,700	4,750	660	40	5,440	140
Men and Women							
Under 25	5,500	1,310	3,430	620	20	4,080	110
25 to 29	1,330	340	730	230	10	970	20
30 to 34	690	200	350	110	10	470	20
35 to 39	710	170	400	120	10	520	20
40 to 44	460	120	270	70	10	340	10
45 to 49	160	30	80	30	-	120	-
50 to 54	40	20	20	10	-	30	-
55 & over	-	-	-	-	-	-	-
Total	8,890	2,190	5,280	1,190	50	6,520	180

Source: Database of Teacher Records.

1. Includes those trained through the Open University.
2. Some in service teachers may be shown as not in service because their service details are not recorded. These may include; entrants to the 'old' university sector, entrants to the independent sector who are not in the Teachers Pension Scheme(TPS), entrants to part-time service outside the maintained nursery, primary and secondary sector who are not in the TPS.
3. Provisional data. The numbers shown as in service may increase as a result of late receipt of annual service returns.

NEW ENTRANTS TO TEACHING

PGCE completers: Calendar year 1999: type of service and sector by sex and age

ENGLAND[1]

	Total PGCE completers England in 1999	Not in service in England 31.3.00[2,3]	In full or part-time service in England on 31 March 2000[3]				
			Maintained nursery and primary	Maintained secondary	Maintained special and PRU	Total maintained schools	FE, HE and independent schools
Men							
Under 25	1,160	310	110	670	-	780	70
25 to 29	1,590	410	190	890	10	1,090	90
30 to 34	660	210	90	320	-	410	40
35 to 39	450	140	60	220	-	280	30
40 to 44	250	80	20	130	-	150	20
45 to 49	150	60	10	60	-	70	20
50 to 54	40	20	-	20	-	20	-
55 & over	10	10	-	-	-	-	-
Total 4,300		1,240	490	2,310	20	2,810	260
Women							
Under 25	4,190	850	1,180	1,970	20	3,170	170
25 to 29	3,600	870	950	1,610	10	2,570	150
30 to 34	1,110	320	290	460	10	760	30
35 to 39	980	280	310	370	10	680	30
40 to 44	700	200	220	250	-	470	30
45 to 49	300	90	50	130	-	180	20
50 to 54	60	30	10	20	-	30	-
55 & over	-	-	-	-	-	-	-
Total 10,940		2,650	3,010	4,800	50	7,860	430
Men and Women							
Under 25	5,350	1,160	1,290	2,630	20	3,950	240
25 to 29	5,190	1,290	1,140	2,500	20	3,660	240
30 to 34	1,770	530	380	790	10	1,180	70
35 to 39	1,430	420	370	580	10	960	50
40 to 44	940	280	240	380	-	620	40
45 to 49	440	150	60	190	-	250	40
50 to 54	100	50	10	40	-	50	-
55 & over	10	10	-	-	-	-	-
Total	15,240	3,890	3,500	7,110	70	10,670	690

Source: Database of Teacher Records.

1. Includes those trained through the Open University.
2. Some in service teachers may be shown as not in service because their service details are not recorded. These may include; entrants to the 'old' university sector, entrants to the independent sector who are not in the Teachers Pension Scheme(TPS), entrants to part-time service outside the maintained nursery, primary and secondary sector who are not in the TPS.
3. Provisional data. The numbers shown as in service may increase as a result of late receipt of annual service returns.

NEW ENTRANTS TO TEACHING
BEd and PGCE completers: Calendar year 1999: type of service and sector by sex and age

ENGLAND[1]

	Total completers England in 1999	Not in service in England 31.3.00[2,3]	In full or part-time service in England on 31 March 2000[3]				
			Maintained nursery and primary	Maintained secondary	Maintained special and PRU	Total maintained schools	FE, HE and independent schools
Men							
Under 25	1,970	550	420	900	10	1,320	90
25 to 29	1,900	500	290	1,010	10	1,300	100
30 to 34	860	280	140	390	10	530	40
35 to 39	600	180	100	280	-	380	30
40 to 44	340	110	50	160	-	210	20
45 to 49	190	70	20	80	-	100	20
50 to 54	50	20	10	20	-	30	-
55 & over	10	10	-	-	-	-	-
Total 5,910	1,720	1,020	2,830	30	3,880	300	
Women							
Under 25	8,880	1,920	4,300	2,360	40	6,700	260
25 to 29	4,620	1,120	1,590	1,720	20	3,330	170
30 to 34	1,600	450	590	510	10	1,110	40
35 to 39	1,540	410	660	420	10	1,100	40
40 to 44	1,070	290	460	280	10	750	30
45 to 49	410	110	130	140	-	270	20
50 to 54	90	40	20	30	-	50	-
55 & over	-	-	-	-	-	-	-
Total 18,220	4,350	7,760	5,460	80	13,310	570	
Men and Women							
Under 25	10,850	2,470	4,730	3,260	40	8,020	360
25 to 29	6,520	1,630	1,880	2,730	30	4,630	260
30 to 34	2,460	730	730	890	20	1,640	80
35 to 39	2,140	590	770	700	10	1,480	70
40 to 44	1,410	400	510	450	10	960	50
45 to 49	600	190	150	220	10	370	40
50 to 54	150	60	30	50	-	80	-
55 & over	10	10	-	-	-	-	-
Total	24,130	6,070	8,780	8,290	110	17,190	870

Source: Database of Teacher Records.

1. Includes those trained through the Open University.
2. Some in service teachers may be shown as not in service because their service details are not recorded. These may include; entrants to the 'old' university sector, entrants to the independent sector who are not in the Teachers Pension Scheme(TPS), entrants to part-time service outside the maintained nursery, primary and secondary sector who are not in the TPS.
3. Provisional data. The numbers shown as in service may increase as a result of late receipt of annual service returns.

NEW ENTRANTS TO TEACHING
Employment based route ITT completers : Calendar year 1999: type of service and sector by sex and age

ENGLAND AND WALES[1]

| | Total employment based route completers in 1999 | Not in service in England and Wales 31.3.00[2,3] | In full or part-time service on 31 March 2000[3] | | | | | | |
| | | | England | | | | | Wales | |
			Maintained nursery and primary	Maintained secondary	Maintained special and PRU	Total maintained schools	FE, HE and Independent schools	Maintained schools sector	FE, HE and Independent schools
Men									
Under 25	-	-	-	-	-	-	-	-	-
25 to 29	30	10	10	10	10	20	-	-	-
30 to 34	30	10	10	10	-	20	-	-	-
35 to 39	20	10	-	10	-	20	-	-	-
40 to 44	10	-	-	-	-	10	-	-	-
45 to 49	10	-	-	10	-	10	-	-	-
50 to 54	10	-	-	-	-	10	-	-	-
55 & over	-	-	-	-	-	-	-	-	-
Total	110	30	20	40	10	70	10	-	-
Women									
Under 25	10	-	-	-	-	10	-	-	-
25 to 29	120	40	30	40	10	80	-	-	-
30 to 34	60	20	20	20	-	40	-	-	-
35 to 39	50	10	10	20	-	40	-	-	-
40 to 44	50	10	20	20	-	40	-	-	-
45 to 49	50	10	20	20	-	40	-	-	-
50 to 54	20	10	-	10	-	10	-	-	-
55 & over	10	-	-	-	-	-	-	-	-
Total	360	80	120	120	20	260	10	10	-
Men and Women									
Under 25	10	-	-	-	-	10	-	-	-
25 to 29	150	40	40	50	20	100	10	-	-
30 to 34	90	30	30	20	10	60	10	-	-
35 to 39	70	10	20	30	-	50	-	-	-
40 to 44	60	10	30	20	-	50	-	-	-
45 to 49	60	10	20	20	-	40	-	-	-
50 to 54	30	10	10	10	-	20	-	-	-
55 & over	10	-	-	-	-	-	-	-	-
Total	470	110	140	160	30	330	20	10	-

Source: Database of Teacher Records.

1. Includes those trained through the Open University.
2. Some in service teachers may be shown as not in service because their service details are not recorded. These may include; entrants to the 'old' university sector, entrants to the independent sector who are not in the Teachers Pension Scheme(TPS), entrants to part-time service outside the maintained nursery, primary and secondary sector who are not in the TPS.
3. Provisional data. The numbers shown as in service may increase as a result of late receipt of annual service returns.

8 NEW ENTRANTS TO TEACHING

ITT completers in calendar year 1999 in full or part-time service in the maintained schools sector at 31 March 2000: region and sector of service by region of ITT

ENGLAND AND WALES[1]

	Region of service at 31 March 2000[2]										
	North East	North West	Yorkshire and The Humber	East Midlands	West Midlands	East of England	London	South East	South West	England	Wales
Region of ITT											
Nursery & Primary											
North East	270	20	20	10	0	0	20	10	-	350	-
North West	40	820	60	50	90	30	70	40	20	1,210	10
Yorkshire and The Humber	50	130	550	70	30	30	30	20	10	910	-
East Midlands	10	30	70	390	80	110	60	60	30	840	-
West Midlands	-	40	20	40	570	40	40	40	20	820	-
East of England	-	10	10	30	20	530	140	60	20	800	-
London	10	10	10	10	10	100	1,050	240	20	1,460	-
South East	-	10	10	20	30	100	130	970	80	1,340	-
South West	-	20	10	20	40	60	90	120	530	870	10
OU and SCITT	10	20	10	10	10	30	20	40	30	180	-
England[1]	400	1,090	750	640	870	1,030	1,660	1,590	760	8,780	20
Wales	-	70	10	20	50	40	60	60	40	370	370
Secondary											
North East	340	20	20	20	10	30	10	20	-	460	-
North West	20	910	70	40	90	60	60	70	30	1,340	30
Yorkshire and The Humber	30	110	610	130	50	60	50	60	20	1,110	10
East Midlands	-	10	10	310	70	50	30	50	20	550	10
West Midlands	-	40	10	40	500	40	30	60	30	750	10
East of England	10	10	10	50	30	430	60	70	30	690	-
London	-	10	-	10	20	140	810	230	20	1,240	-
South East	-	10	10	20	20	70	90	680	80	990	-
South West	-	10	10	20	50	60	50	160	560	900	30
OU and SCITT	10	20	10	20	70	40	10	40	30	250	10
England[1]	420	1,130	780	640	910	980	1,200	1,430	820	8,290	100
Wales	-	20	10	10	30	20	20	50	50	210	390
Special and PRU											
North East	20	-	-	-	-	-	-	-	-	20	-
North West	-	10	-	-	-	-	-	-	-	20	-
Yorkshire and The Humber	-	-	10	-	-	-	-	-	-	10	-
East Midlands	-	-	-	-	-	-	-	-	-	10	-
West Midlands	-	-	-	-	10	-	-	-	-	20	-
East of England	-	-	-	-	-	10	-	-	-	10	-
London	-	-	-	-	-	-	10	-	-	20	-
South East	-	-	-	-	-	-	-	10	-	10	-
South West	-	-	-	-	-	-	-	-	10	10	-
OU and SCITT	-	-	-	-	-	-	-	-	-	-	-
England[1]	20	10	10	10	20	20	10	10	10	110	-
Wales	-	-	-	-	-	-	-	-	-	-	10

Source: Database of Teacher Records.

1. Includes those trained through the Open University.
2. Provisonal data. The numbers shown as in service may increase as a result of late receipt of annual service returns.

NEW ENTRANTS TO TEACHING

ITT completers in calendar year 1999 teaching full-time in the maintained schools sector in March 2000 by salary range, average salary, phase, sex and age[1,2]

ENGLAND AND WALES

	Not Known	up to £14,999	£15,000 -£16,999	£17,000 -£18,999	£19,000 and over	Total	Average salary (£)
Nursery and primary							
Men							
Under 25	20	20	370	70	-	480	15,850
25-29	20	10	230	60	10	320	16,120
30-34	10	-	90	50	10	150	16,680
35-39	10	-	60	30	10	100	16,750
40-49	-	-	40	20	-	60	16,670
50 and over	-	-	-	-	-	-	17,110
All ages	60	30	780	220	30	1,120	16,170
Women							
Under 25	280	100	3,580	720	10	4,670	15,910
25-29	90	20	1,170	370	20	1,670	16,180
30-34	40	10	360	150	30	590	16,480
35-39	40	10	400	150	30	640	16,490
40-49	50	20	330	110	40	550	16,540
50 and over	-	-	10	10	-	20	16,930
All ages	500	170	5,850	1,500	130	8,140	16,090
Men and Women	560	190	6,630	1,720	160	9,260	16,100
Secondary							
Men							
Under 25	70	50	720	100	-	950	15,830
25-29	80	40	730	170	20	1,040	16,230
30-34	20	10	190	140	30	390	16,930
35-39	20	10	110	90	50	280	17,500
40-49	20	10	70	70	60	230	17,990
50 and over	-	-	10	10	10	20	19,050
All ages	210	120	1,820	580	180	2,910	16,480
Women							
Under 25	140	80	1,940	310	10	2,490	15,850
25-29	120	60	1,240	290	30	1,740	16,140
30-34	50	10	230	150	40	490	16,890
35-39	30	10	170	110	30	350	16,890
40-49	40	20	160	80	50	340	17,130
50 and over	-	-	10	-	-	20	17,780
All ages	380	180	3,760	940	160	5,420	16,180
Men and Women	600	300	5,580	1,520	340	8,330	16,290
Special and PRU							
Men	-	-	20	10	-	30	17,040
Women	-	-	50	20	10	90	17,110
Men and Women	10	-	70	30	10	120	17,090
Maintained schools sector							
Men	270	150	2,620	800	210	4,060	16,400
Women	880	340	9,650	2,470	300	13,640	16,140
Men and Women	1,160	490	12,270	3,270	510	17,700	16,200

Source: Database of Teacher Records.

1. Provisional data. The numbers shown as in service may change as a result of late receipt of annual service returns.
2. Includes some teachers projected as entering full-time service, but whose salary is not known and hence excluded from the average salary calculation.

9b

NEW ENTRANTS TO TEACHING
ITT completers in calendar year 1999 teaching full-time in the maintained schools sector in March 2000 by salary range, average salary, phase, sex and age[1,2]

ENGLAND

	Not Known	up to £14,999	£15,000 -£16,999	£17,000 -£18,999	£19,000 and over	Total	Average salary (£)
Nursery and primary							
Men							
Under 25	20	20	350	70	-	450	15,880
25-29	20	-	210	60	10	300	16,160
30-34	10	-	80	50	10	140	16,720
35-39	10	-	60	20	10	100	16,750
40-49	-	-	30	20	-	60	16,670
50 and over	-	-	-	-	-	-	17,110
All ages	50	20	730	220	30	1,060	16,200
Women							
Under 25	250	90	3,410	720	10	4,480	15,920
25-29	90	20	1,130	370	20	1,620	16,200
30-34	40	10	350	150	30	580	16,500
35-39	40	10	380	150	30	620	16,510
40-49	40	20	320	110	40	530	16,560
50 and over	-	-	10	10	-	20	16,930
All ages	460	160	5,600	1,500	130	7,840	16,110
Men and Women	510	180	6,330	1,720	160	8,900	16,120
Secondary							
Men							
Under 25	70	50	680	100	-	900	15,840
25-29	70	40	700	160	20	1,000	16,250
30-34	20	10	180	140	30	380	16,960
35-39	20	10	110	90	50	270	17,490
40-49	10	10	70	70	60	220	18,050
50 and over	-	-	10	10	10	20	19,050
All ages	200	110	1,740	560	170	2,780	16,500
Women							
Under 25	120	80	1,830	310	10	2,340	15,870
25-29	120	50	1,190	280	30	1,680	16,160
30-34	50	10	220	150	40	460	16,920
35-39	30	10	160	110	30	330	16,940
40-49	30	10	160	80	50	340	17,150
50 and over	-	-	10	-	-	20	17,950
All ages	340	160	3,560	940	160	5,160	16,210
Men and Women	540	270	5,300	1,500	340	7,940	16,310
Special and PRU							
Men	-	-	20	-	-	30	17,080
Women	-	-	50	20	10	80	17,150
Men and Women	10	-	60	30	10	110	17,130
Maintained schools sector							
Men	250	140	2,490	790	210	3,860	16,420
Women	810	320	9,210	2,460	290	13,080	16,160
Men and Women	1,060	460	11,690	3,240	500	16,950	16,220

Source: Database of Teacher Records.

1. Provisional data. The numbers shown as in service may change as a result of late receipt of annual service returns.
2. Includes some teachers projected as entering full-time service, but whose salary is not known and hence excluded from the average salary calculation.

NEW ENTRANTS TO TEACHING

10

ITT completers in calendar year 1999 teaching full-time in the maintained schools sector in March 2000 by region of service, sex and age[1]

ENGLAND AND WALES

	North East	North West	Yorkshire and The Humber	East Midlands	West Midlands	East of England	London	South East	South West	England	Wales	England and Wales
Men												
Under 25	70	190	120	110	150	170	180	250	120	1,350	80	1,440
25-29	70	190	110	90	120	140	220	230	140	1,300	60	1,370
30-34	20	70	40	40	60	40	110	100	50	530	20	550
35-39	20	50	40	40	40	30	60	60	40	370	20	390
40-49	10	30	30	20	30	40	30	70	30	290	10	300
50 and over	0	0	0	0	0	0	0	10	0	30	0	30
All ages	190	530	340	290	400	430	600	700	380	3,860	200	4,060
Women												
Under 25	330	910	600	510	820	860	1,090	1,170	560	6,850	350	7,200
25-29	150	390	260	240	320	380	660	590	320	3,320	110	3,420
30-34	40	130	110	70	100	100	220	190	90	1,050	50	1,090
35-39	40	110	90	80	100	130	160	160	90	960	40	990
40-49	50	110	60	60	60	120	150	200	70	880	20	900
50 and over	0	0	0	0	0	10	10	10	0	40	0	40
All ages	610	1,660	1,130	970	1,390	1,590	2,280	2,320	1,120	13,080	560	13,640
Men and Women												
Under 25	400	1,100	720	620	970	1,030	1,270	1,420	680	8,210	430	8,640
25-29	220	580	370	330	440	520	880	820	460	4,620	170	4,790
30-34	70	210	150	110	150	140	330	280	130	1,570	70	1,640
35-39	60	160	130	110	140	160	210	220	120	1,330	50	1,380
40-49	60	140	90	80	90	160	180	270	100	1,170	30	1,200
50 and over	10	0	10	10	0	10	10	10	10	60	0	60
All ages	800	2,190	1,470	1,260	1,790	2,020	2,880	3,030	1,500	16,950	750	17,700

Source: Database of Teacher Records.

1. Provisional data. The numbers shown as in service may change as a result of late receipt of annual service returns.

TEACHER FLOWS (INFLOW)
Maintained schools sector: full-time qualified teacher joiners by age[1], sex and type of flow, 31 March 1999 to 31 March 2000 (provisional)

ENGLAND

	Under 25	25-29	30-34	35-39	40-44	45-49	50-54	55-59	60 and over	Total
Nursery and Primary										
Men										
New entrants[2]	500	300	100	100	-	-	-	-	-	1,100
New to maintained sector[3]	-	100	100	-	-	-	-	-	-	300
Returner to maintained sector[4]	-	100	100	100	100	100	-	-	-	400
Total inflow[5]	500	500	300	200	100	100	100	-	-	1,800
Women										
New entrants[2]	4,500	1,700	600	600	400	100	-	-	-	8,000
New to maintained sector[3]	400	600	200	200	300	300	100	-	-	2,100
Returner to maintained sector[4]	-	500	400	300	400	400	200	100	-	2,300
Total inflow[5]	4,900	2,700	1,200	1,200	1,100	800	400	100	-	12,500
Men and women										
New entrants[2]	4,900	2,000	800	700	500	200	-	-	-	9,100
New to maintained sector[3]	400	700	300	200	300	300	200	100	-	2,500
Returner to maintained sector[4]	-	500	500	400	400	500	300	100	-	2,700
Total inflow[5]	5,400	3,200	1,500	1,400	1,200	1,000	500	200	-	14,200
Secondary										
Men										
New entrants[2]	900	1,000	400	300	200	100	-	-	-	2,900
New to maintained sector[3]	100	300	200	100	100	100	100	-	-	1,200
Returner to maintained sector[4]	-	200	200	100	100	200	100	100	-	1,000
Total inflow[5]	1,000	1,500	800	600	400	400	200	100	-	5,000
Women										
New entrants[2]	2,400	1,800	500	400	200	100	-	-	-	5,300
New to maintained sector[3]	200	500	200	200	200	200	100	-	-	1,700
Returner to maintained sector[4]	-	300	200	200	200	200	100	100	-	1,400
Total inflow[5]	2,600	2,600	1,000	700	700	600	300	100	-	8,400
Men and women										
New entrants[2]	3,300	2,800	900	600	400	200	-	-	-	8,200
New to maintained sector[3]	300	900	500	300	300	300	200	100	-	2,900
Returner to maintained sector[4]	-	500	400	300	400	400	300	100	-	2,400
Total inflow[5]	3,600	4,100	1,800	1,300	1,100	900	500	200	100	13,500

11a(i)

TEACHER FLOWS (INFLOW)

Maintained schools sector: full-time qualified teacher joiners by age[1], sex and type of flow, 31 March 1999 to 31 March 2000 (provisional)

ENGLAND

	Under 25	25-29	30-34	35-39	40-44	45-49	50-54	55-59	60 and over	Total
Other maintained schools[6]										
Men										
New entrants[2]	-	-	-	-	-	-	-	-	-	-
New to maintained sector[3]	-	-	-	-	-	-	-	-	-	100
Returner to maintained sector[4]	-	-	-	-	-	-	-	-	-	100
Total inflow[5]	-	-	-	-	-	-	-	-	-	200
Women										
New entrants[2]	-	-	-	-	-	-	-	-	-	100
New to maintained sector[3]	-	-	-	-	-	-	-	-	-	200
Returner to maintained sector[4]	-	-	-	-	-	100	-	-	-	200
Total inflow[5]	-	100	100	100	100	100	100	-	-	500
Men and women										
New entrants[2]	-	-	-	-	-	-	-	-	-	100
New to maintained sector[3]	-	-	-	-	100	100	-	-	-	300
Returner to maintained sector[4]	-	-	-	-	100	100	100	-	-	300
Total inflow[5]	100	100	100	100	100	100	100	-	-	700
Total										
Men										
New entrants[2]	1,400	1,300	600	400	200	100	-	-	-	4,000
New to maintained sector[3]	100	500	300	200	200	200	100	-	-	1,600
Returner to maintained sector[4]	-	200	300	200	200	200	200	100	-	1,400
Total inflow[5]	1,500	2,000	1,100	800	600	500	300	100	-	7,000
Women										
New entrants[2]	6,900	3,500	1,100	1,000	700	300	100	-	-	13,500
New to maintained sector[3]	500	1,100	500	400	500	600	300	100	-	4,000
Returner to maintained sector[4]	100	800	600	600	600	700	400	100	-	4,000
Total inflow[5]	7,500	5,400	2,200	1,900	1,800	1,500	700	300	100	21,400
Men and women										
New entrants[2]	8,300	4,800	1,700	1,400	900	400	100	-	-	17,400
New to maintained sector[3]	700	1,600	800	600	700	700	400	100	-	5,600
Returner to maintained sector[4]	100	1,000	900	800	800	900	600	200	100	5,400
Total inflow[5]	9,000	7,400	3,400	2,700	2,400	2,000	1,100	400	100	28,400

Source: Database of Teacher Records.

1. Age as at 31 March 2000.
2. Teacher qualified in 1999.
3. Teacher has no known service in the English maintained schools sector, and qualified before 1999.
4. Teacher was not in service last year, but has previous service in the English maintained schools sector.
5. Does not include joiners from part-time service (of whom there were 4,500 in the whole maintained sector-see table 11c) or from other parts of the English maintained schools sector (900 moved to primary schools, 1,000 moved to secondary schools, 600 moved to other maintained schools. 200 of these also moved from part-time to full-time). It does include joiners from the FE, HE and independent sectors and Wales.
6. Includes maintained special schools and PRUs.

TEACHER FLOWS (INFLOW)

Maintained schools sector: part-time[1] qualified teacher joiners by age[2], sex and type of flow, 31 March 1999 to 31 March 2000 (provisional)

ENGLAND

	Under 25	25-29	30-34	35-39	40-44	45-49	50-54	55-59	60 and over	Total
Nursery and Primary										
Men										
New entrants[3]	-	-	-	-	-	-	-	-	-	-
New to maintained sector[4]	-	-	-	-	-	-	-	-	-	100
Returner to maintained sector[5]	-	-	-	-	-	-	-	-	-	100
Total inflow[6]	-	-	-	-	-	-	100	-	-	200
Women										
New entrants[3]	100	-	-	100	100	-	-	-	-	300
New to maintained sector[4]	-	100	100	200	300	300	200	100	-	1,400
Returner to maintained sector[5]	-	100	300	300	400	400	200	100	100	1,900
Total inflow[6]	100	200	400	600	800	700	400	200	100	3,500
Men and women										
New entrants[3]	100	-	-	100	100	-	-	-	-	300
New to maintained sector[4]	-	100	100	200	300	300	200	100	-	1,400
Returner to maintained sector[5]	-	100	300	300	400	400	200	200	100	2,000
Total inflow[6]	100	200	400	600	800	700	500	300	100	3,700
Secondary										
Men										
New entrants[3]	-	-	-	-	-	-	-	-	-	100
New to maintained sector[4]	-	-	-	-	-	-	100	-	-	300
Returner to maintained sector[5]	-	-	-	-	-	-	100	100	100	500
Total inflow[6]	-	100	100	100	100	100	200	200	100	900
Women										
New entrants[3]	100	100	-	100	100	-	-	-	-	400
New to maintained sector[4]	-	100	100	200	200	200	200	100	-	1,100
Returner to maintained sector[5]	-	-	100	200	300	300	200	200	100	1,500
Total inflow[6]	100	200	300	500	600	500	400	200	100	2,900
Men and women										
New entrants[3]	100	100	100	100	100	-	-	-	-	500
New to maintained sector[4]	-	100	100	200	300	300	200	100	-	1,400
Returner to maintained sector[5]	-	-	200	300	400	300	300	300	200	2,000
Total inflow[6]	100	200	300	500	700	600	600	400	200	3,800

CONTINUED
TEACHER FLOWS (INFLOW)
Maintained schools sector: part-time[1] qualified teacher joiners by age[2], sex and type of flow, 31 March 1999 to 31 March 2000 (provisional)

ENGLAND

	Under 25	25-29	30-34	35-39	40-44	45-49	50-54	55-59	60 and over	Total
Other maintained schools[7]										
Men										
New entrants[3]	-	-	-	-	-	-	-	-	-	-
New to maintained sector[4]	-	-	-	-	-	-	-	-	-	-
Returner to maintained sector[5]	-	-	-	-	-	-	-	-	-	-
Total inflow[6]	-	-	-	-	-	-	-	-	-	100
Women										
New entrants[3]	-	-	-	-	-	-	-	-	-	-
New to maintained sector[4]	-	-	-	-	-	-	-	-	-	100
Returner to maintained sector[5]	-	-	-	-	-	-	-	-	-	200
Total inflow[6]	-	-	-	-	100	100	-	-	-	300
Men and women										
New entrants[3]	-	-	-	-	-	-	-	-	-	-
New to maintained sector[4]	-	-	-	-	-	-	-	-	-	100
Returner to maintained sector[5]	-	-	-	-	-	-	-	-	-	200
Total inflow[6]	-	-	-	-	100	100	100	-	-	300
Total										
Men										
New entrants[3]	-	-	-	-	-	-	-	-	-	100
New to maintained sector[4]	-	-	-	-	100	-	100	100	-	400
Returner to maintained sector[5]	-	-	-	100	-	100	200	200	100	700
Total inflow[6]	-	100	100	100	100	100	300	200	100	1,200
Women										
New entrants[3]	100	100	100	100	100	-	-	-	-	600
New to maintained sector[4]	-	100	200	400	600	600	400	200	100	2,500
Returner to maintained sector[5]	-	100	400	600	800	700	500	300	200	3,500
Total inflow[6]	100	400	700	1,100	1,500	1,300	900	500	200	6,700
Men and women										
New entrants[3]	200	100	100	200	100	100	-	-	-	800
New to maintained sector[4]	-	200	300	400	600	600	500	200	100	2,900
Returner to maintained sector[5]	-	100	400	600	800	700	600	500	300	4,200
Total inflow[6]	200	400	800	1,200	1,600	1,400	1,100	700	400	7,900

Source: Database of Teacher Records.

1. 10-20% of part-time teachers may not be included in the data.
2. Age as at 31 March 2000.
3. Teacher qualified in 1999.
4. Teacher has no known service in the English maintained schools sector, and qualified before 1999.
5. Teacher was not in service last year, but has previous service in the English maintained schools sector.
6. Does not include joiners from full-time service (of whom there were 6,600 in the whole maintained sector-see table 11c) or from other parts of the English maintained schools sector (400 moved to primary schools, 400 moved to secondary schools, 100 moved to other maintained schools). 300 of these also moved from full-time to part-time. It does include joiners from the FE, HE and independent sectors and Wales.
7. Includes maintained special schools and PRUs.

11b(i)

TEACHER FLOWS (OUTFLOW)
Maintained schools sector: full-time qualified teacher wastage by age[1], sex and type of flow, 31 March 1999 to 31 March 2000 (provisional)

ENGLAND

	Under 25	25-29	30-34	35-39	40-44	45-49	50-54	55-59	60 and over	Total
Nursery and Primary										
Men										
Out of service[2]	-	200	200	200	200	200	200	100	-	1,400
Retired	-	-	-	-	-	100	200	200	100	600
Total outflow[3]	-	200	200	200	200	300	400	200	200	2,000
Women										
Out of service[2]	200	2,000	1,500	900	800	1,200	1,100	500	100	8,200
Retired	-	-	-	-	-	200	600	600	900	2,300
Total outflow[3]	200	2,000	1,500	900	800	1,300	1,600	1,100	1,000	10,500
Men and women										
Out of service[2]	300	2,200	1,700	1,100	1,000	1,400	1,300	500	100	9,600
Retired	-	-	-	-	-	200	800	800	1,100	3,000
Total outflow[3]	300	2,200	1,700	1,100	1,000	1,600	2,100	1,400	1,100	12,500
Secondary										
Men										
Out of service[2]	100	700	600	500	500	600	500	100	-	3,500
Retired	-	-	-	-	-	100	600	400	400	1,600
Total outflow[3]	100	700	600	500	500	700	1,000	600	500	5,100
Women										
Out of service[2]	200	1,400	1,000	600	600	700	500	200	-	5,200
Retired	-	-	-	-	-	100	300	300	500	1,300
Total outflow[3]	200	1,400	1,000	600	600	800	800	500	500	6,500
Men and women										
Out of service[2]	200	2,100	1,600	1,100	1,100	1,300	1,000	300	-	8,700
Retired	-	-	-	-	-	200	900	800	1,000	2,900
Total outflow[3]	200	2,100	1,600	1,100	1,100	1,500	1,900	1,100	1,000	11,600

CONTINUED
TEACHER FLOWS (OUTFLOW)

11b(i)

Maintained schools sector: full-time qualified teacher wastage by age[1], sex and type of flow, 31 March 1999 to 31 March 2000 (provisional)

ENGLAND

	Under 25	25-29	30-34	35-39	40-44	45-49	50-54	55-59	60 and over	Total
Other maintained schools[4]										
Men										
Out of service[2]	-	-	-	-	-	100	-	-	-	200
Retired	-	-	-	-	-	-	-	-	-	100
Total outflow[3]	-	-	-	-	-	100	100	-	-	300
Women										
Out of service[2]	-	-	100	100	100	100	100	-	-	500
Retired	-	-	-	-	-	-	-	100	100	200
Total outflow[3]	-	-	100	100	100	100	100	100	100	600
Men and women										
Out of service[2]	-	-	100	100	100	200	100	-	-	700
Retired	-	-	-	-	-	-	100	100	100	300
Total outflow[3]	-	-	100	100	100	200	200	100	100	1,000
Total										
Men										
Out of service[2]	100	900	800	700	700	900	700	200	-	5,100
Retired	-	-	-	-	-	200	800	700	600	2,300
Total outflow[3]	100	900	800	700	700	1,100	1,500	900	700	7,500
Women										
Out of service[2]	400	3,400	2,600	1,600	1,500	2,000	1,700	700	100	13,800
Retired	-	-	-	-	100	300	900	1,000	1,500	3,800
Total outflow[3]	400	3,400	2,600	1,600	1,500	2,300	2,600	1,700	1,600	17,700
Men and women										
Out of service[2]	500	4,400	3,400	2,300	2,100	2,900	2,400	900	100	19,000
Retired	-	-	-	-	100	400	1,700	1,700	2,100	6,100
Total outflow[3]	500	4,400	3,400	2,300	2,200	3,400	4,100	2,600	2,200	25,100

Source: Database of Teacher Records.

1. Age as at 31 March 2000.
2. Teacher is not in service in the English maintained sector and is not receiving a pension. May be teaching in FE/HE sectors or Wales.
3. Does not include wastage to part-time service (of whom there were 6,600 in the whole maintained sector-see table 11c) or from other parts of the English maintained schools sector (1,100 left from primary schools, 1,100 left from secondary schools, 400 left from other maintained schools. 300 of these also moved from full-time to part-time). It does include wastage to the FE, HE and independent sectors and Wales.
4. Includes maintained special schools and PRUs.

11b(ii)

TEACHER FLOWS (OUTFLOW)
Maintained schools sector: part-time[1] qualified teacher wastage by age[2], sex and type of flow, 31 March 1999 to 31 March 2000 (provisional)

ENGLAND

	Under 25	25-29	30-34	35-39	40-44	45-49	50-54	55-59	60 and over	Total
Nursery and Primary										
Men										
Out of service[3]	-	-	-	-	-	-	-	-	-	100
Retired	-	-	-	-	-	-	-	-	100	100
Total outflow[4]	-	-	-	-	-	-	-	100	100	200
Women										
Out of service[3]	-	100	500	500	600	800	600	200	100	3,400
Retired	-	-	-	-	-	-	100	200	400	800
Total outflow[4]	-	100	500	500	600	800	700	500	500	4,200
Men and women										
Out of service[3]	-	100	500	600	600	800	600	200	100	3,500
Retired	-	-	-	-	-	-	200	300	500	1,000
Total outflow[4]	-	100	500	600	600	800	800	500	600	4,500
Secondary										
Men										
Out of service[3]	-	-	100	100	100	100	100	-	-	500
Retired	-	-	-	-	-	-	200	300	300	800
Total outflow[4]	-	-	100	100	100	100	300	300	300	1,200
Women										
Out of service[3]	-	100	300	500	600	600	500	200	100	2,800
Retired	-	-	-	-	-	-	100	300	400	800
Total outflow[4]	-	100	300	500	600	600	600	500	400	3,700
Men and women										
Out of service[3]	-	200	400	500	600	700	600	200	100	3,300
Retired	-	-	-	-	-	-	300	600	700	1,600
Total outflow[4]	-	200	400	500	700	700	900	900	700	4,900

11b(ii)

TEACHER FLOWS (OUTFLOW)

Maintained schools sector: part-time[1] qualified teacher wastage by age[2], sex and type of flow, 31 March 1999 to 31 March 2000 (provisional)

ENGLAND

	Under 25	25-29	30-34	35-39	40-44	45-49	50-54	55-59	60 and over	Total
Other maintained schools[5]										
Men										
Out of service[3]	-	-	-	-	-	-	-	-	-	-
Retired	-	-	-	-	-	-	-	-	-	-
Total outflow[4]	-	-	-	-	-	-	-	-	-	100
Women										
Out of service[3]	-	-	-	-	-	100	-	-	-	300
Retired	-	-	-	-	-	-	-	-	-	100
Total outflow[4]	-	-	-	-	-	100	100	100	-	300
Men and women										
Out of service[3]	-	-	-	-	-	100	100	-	-	300
Retired	-	-	-	-	-	-	-	100	100	100
Total outflow[4]	-	-	-	-	-	100	100	100	100	400
Total										
Men										
Out of service[3]	-	-	100	100	100	100	100	100	-	600
Retired	-	-	-	-	-	-	200	400	400	900
Total outflow[4]	-	-	100	100	100	100	300	400	400	1,600
Women										
Out of service[3]	-	200	800	1,000	1,200	1,400	1,100	500	100	6,500
Retired	-	-	-	-	-	-	300	600	800	1,800
Total outflow[4]	-	200	800	1,000	1,300	1,500	1,400	1,000	1,000	8,300
Men and women										
Out of service[3]	-	300	900	1,100	1,300	1,600	1,200	500	200	7,100
Retired	-	-	-	-	-	100	500	900	1,200	2,700
Total outflow[4]	-	300	900	1,100	1,400	1,600	1,700	1,500	1,400	9,800

Source: Database of Teacher Records.

1. 10-20% of part-time teachers may not be included in the data.
2. Age as at 31 March 2000.
3. Teacher is not in service in the English maintained sector and is not receiving a pension. May be teaching in FE/HE sectors or Wales.
4. Does not include wastage to full-time service (of whom there were 4,500 in the whole maintained sector-see table 11c) or from other parts of the English maintained schools sector (400 left from primary schools,400 left from secondary schools, 100 left from other maintained schools. 200 of these also moved from part-time to full-time). It does include wastage to the FE, HE and independent sectors and Wales.
5. Includes maintained special schools and PRUs.

TEACHER FLOWS

11c

Maintained schools sector: 1989-90, 1994-95, 1997-98, 1998-99 and 1999-2000[1]; qualified teacher joiners and wastage by type and destination[2]

ENGLAND

	1989-90	1994-95	1997-98	1998-99	1999-2000[1]
Full-time					
Entrants to full-time teaching in the maintained schools sector					
New entrants to teaching	12,700	16,600	18,000	16,800	17,400
New to maintained sector	4,900	4,600	5,800	5,100	5,600
Returner to maintained sector	8,500	6,600	5,300	5,100	5,400
Total entrants	26,100	27,800	29,100	27,000	28,400
Joiners from part-time service [3]	*5,400*	*5,000*	*4,900*	*4,600*	*4,500*
Movement from full-time teaching in the maintained schools sector					
Out of service	20,000	13,300	15,700	16,900	19,000
Retired	12,100	12,000	13,800	5,700	6,100
Total wastage	32,100	25,300	29,500	22,600	25,100
Leavers to part-time service [4]	*5,000*	*5,200*	*6,900*	*6,700*	*6,600*
Part-time					
Entrants to part-time teaching in the maintained schools sector					
New entrants to teaching	500	800	900	800	800
New to maintained sector	2,200	2,100	2,700	2,900	2,900
Returner to maintained sector	9,700	6,300	5,200	4,900	4,200
Total entrants	12,400	9,200	8,800	8,600	7,900
Joiners from full-time service [4]	*5,000*	*5,200*	*6,900*	*6,700*	*6,600*
Movement from part-time teaching in the maintained schools sector					
Out of service	6,800	6,600	6,800	6,600	7,100
Retired	800	2,000	2,800	2,400	2,700
Total wastage	7,600	8,500	9,600	9,000	9,800
Leavers to full-time service [3]	*5,400*	*5,000*	*4,900*	*4,600*	*4,500*

Source: Database of Teacher Records.

1. Provisional estimates.
2. 10-20% of part-time teachers may not be included in the data.
3. Full-time joiners from part-time service are equivalent to leavers from part-time to full-time service. Not included in total entrants or total wastage.
4. Part-time joiners from full-time service are equivalent to leavers from full-time to part-time service. Not included in total entrants or total wastage.

TEACHER FLOWS

12 Turnover and wastage rates of qualified teachers by Government Office region, 1998-1999

ENGLAND   (percentages)

Government Office region	Full-time		Part-time[1]	
	Turnover rate[2]	Wastage rate[3]	Turnover rate[4]	Wastage rate[5]
North East	11.4	6.2	31.4	26.6
North West	11.4	6.6	29.0	25.2
Yorkshire and The Humber	11.4	6.5	26.2	23.0
East Midlands	13.5	7.8	30.1	25.9
West Midlands	13.8	7.3	32.3	26.8
East of England	15.8	8.9	32.7	25.7
London	18.4	10.4	27.2	22.6
Of which :				
Inner London	19.3	10.8	28.8	23.1
Outer London	18.1	10.2	26.4	22.3
South East	16.3	9.7	31.7	26.6
South West	14.7	9.0	30.2	26.0
England	14.3	8.2	30.1	25.3
England 1999-2000[6]	14.9	8.8	30.1	26.0

Source: Database of Teacher Records.

1. 10-20% of part-time teachers may not be included in the data.
2. Full-time turnover is defined as all teachers in full-time service in the English maintained schools sector on 31 March 1998 who were not in full-time service in the same establishment on 31 March 1999 (where a teacher moves from a school with a local education authority maintained establishment number to a school with a grant-maintained establishment number within the same local authority, it is assumed that the teacher is in the same school but that it has changed to grant-maintained status). Turnover therefore includes wastage, transfers to other establishments within the maintained schools sector and teachers leaving to part-time service. Not all employers record all movements between schools within their employ so rates are underestimated.
3. Full-time wastage is defined as all teachers in full-time service in the English maintained schools sector on 31 March 1998 who were not in full-time service anywhere in the maintained schools sector on 31 March 1998. This includes teachers leaving to part-time service.
4. Part-time turnover is defined as all teachers in part-time service in the English maintained schools sector on 31 March 1998 who were not in part-time service in the same establishment on 31 March 1999 (where a teacher moves from a school with a local education authority maintained establishment number to a school with a grant-maintained establishment number within the same local authority, it is assumed that the teacher is in the same school but that it has changed to grant-maintained status). Turnover therefore includes wastage, transfers to other establishments within the maintained schools sector and teachers leaving to full-time service. Not all employers record all movements between schools within their employ so rates are underestimated.
5. Part-time wastage is defined as all teachers in part-time service in the English maintained schools sector on 31 March 1998 who were not in part-time service anywhere in the maintained schools sector on 31 March 1998. This includes teachers leaving to full-time service.
6. Provisional data. Rates are not shown by government office region beacause figures have been projected for some LEAs which had not sent returns. This may disproportionately affect some regions.

13

TEACHER FLOWS
Qualified teacher entrants and leavers by Government Office region, English maintained schools sector, 1998 to 1999

ENGLAND

	Total full-time teachers March 1998	All leaving full-time service[1]	Total Entrants[2]	Movement between regions[3]	Total full-time teachers March 1999
England	357,590	29,260	31,560	0	359,890
North East	20,580	1,280	1,440	-10	20,730
North West	55,130	3,620	3,780	-30	55,260
Yorkshire and The Humber	37,510	2,430	2,730	40	37,860
East Midlands	29,590	2,300	2,610	10	29,900
West Midlands	41,860	3,070	3,730	20	42,550
East of England	38,690	3,440	3,610	-30	38,830
London	48,290	5,010	5,280	-310	48,250
South East	53,500	5,210	5,490	100	53,880
South West	32,430	2,910	2,900	210	32,630

	Total part-time teachers March 1998[4]	All leaving part-time service[5]	Total Entrants[6]	Movement between regions[7]	Total part-time teachers March 1999[4]
England	53,520	13,550	15,270	0	55,240
North East	1,710	460	510	0	1,770
North West	6,030	1,520	1,680	0	6,190
Yorkshire and The Humber	4,970	1,140	1,190	0	5,020
East Midlands	4,550	1,180	1,720	-10	5,090
West Midlands	5,380	1,440	1,690	0	5,620
East of England	7,350	1,890	1,940	10	7,400
London	7,700	1,740	1,760	-20	7,690
South East	9,490	2,530	2,780	10	9,750
South West	6,360	1,660	2,000	10	6,720

Source: Database of Teacher Records.

1. Includes teachers leaving to part-time teaching, non-maintained sectors, Wales and retirements.
2. Includes teachers coming from part-time teaching, non-maintained sectors, Wales and retirements.
3. Net imports (positive numbers) indicate inflow of full-time teachers from other regions, net exports (negative numbers) indicate an outflow.
4. 10-20% of part-time teachers may not be included in the data.
5. Includes teachers leaving to full-time teaching, non-maintained sectors, Wales and retirements.
6. Includes teachers coming from full-time teaching, non-maintained sectors, Wales and retirements.
7. Net imports (positive numbers) indicate inflow of part-time teachers from other regions, net exports (negative numbers) indicate an outflow.

TEACHERS IN SERVICE

14

Teacher numbers: 1996 to 2001 by sector and type of service

ENGLAND

	January					
	1996	1997	1998	1999	2000	2001
Nursery and primary						
Qualified teachers	198,530	198,970	197,290	198,810	202,160	204,580
Full-time						
In regular service	176,180	175,750	173,900	173,890	174,720	174,630
On secondment[1]	140	130	90	120	170	120
In occasional service	7,660	8,310	8,290	8,920	10,520	11,960
FTE of part-time	14,550	14,780	15,000	15,880	16,750	17,870
Teachers without QTS[2]	1,050	1,010	1,110	1,230	1,460	2,350
Total teachers	199,570	199,980	198,400	200,040	203,620	206,920
Secondary						
Qualified teachers	191,950	192,050	191,660	194,190	196,420	200,310
Full-time						
In regular service	174,420	174,240	173,840	175,630	176,520	179,110
On secondment[1]	50	40	30	40	110	50
In occasional service	4,120	4,390	3,990	4,460	5,320	6,550
FTE of part-time	13,360	13,370	13,800	14,050	14,460	14,600
Teachers without QTS[2]	1,810	1,770	1,910	2,050	2,100	2,920
Total teachers	193,760	193,820	193,570	196,240	198,520	203,230
Special schools						
Qualified teachers	15,580	15,380	14,930	14,790	14,810	14,850
Full-time						
In regular service	13,790	13,490	13,050	12,880	12,810	12,690
On secondment[1]	40	30	10	10	30	10
In occasional service	630	680	670	640	690	820
FTE of part-time	1,120	1,180	1,210	1,260	1,280	1,320
Teachers without QTS[2]	110	150	170	230	210	300
Total teachers	15,690	15,520	15,100	15,020	15,020	15,150
Education elsewhere[3]						
Qualified teachers	3,360	3,450	3,710	3,060	4,100	4,410
Full-time						
In regular service	2,550	2,550	2,780	3,060	3,100	3,280
On secondment[1]	-	-	-	-	-	-
In occasional service	180	230	190	100	140	260
FTE of part-time	630	670	730	790	860	870
Teachers without QTS[2]	10	10	30	30	40	50
Total teachers	3,370	3,460	3,740	3,980	4,140	4,460
Total[3]	412,390	412,790	410,800	415,280	421,290	429,760
All regular teachers (excluding occasional teachers)	399,790	399,180	397,650	401,160	404,630	410,170

Source: DfES annual 618G survey.

1. For periods of one term or more.
2. Teachers without Qualified Teacher Status, full-time and FTE of part-time.
3. Includes Pupil Referral Units.

15 TEACHERS IN SERVICE

Full-time teachers in maintained secondary schools — teaching-contact ratios[1] by type of teacher

ENGLAND

	Timetabled teaching as percentage of timetabled week
Type of teacher:	
Head teacher	16
Deputy head	38
Other qualified teacher	76
Unqualified teacher	73
Full-time teachers	74
Full-time teachers (excluding head teachers and deputy head teachers)	76

Source : 1996/97 Secondary Schools Curriculum and Staffing Survey

1. Restricted to teachers teaching at least one period per week.

16 Full-time equivalent[1] regular[2] teacher numbers 2001: by sector and Government Office region

ENGLAND AND WALES

Government Office region:	Nursery and primary[3]	Secondary[3]	Special	Elsewhere	Total
North East	10,350	11,070	840	290	22,540
North West	29,010	28,480	2,310	580	60,380
Yorkshire and The Humber	20,720	20,590	1,290	430	43,030
East Midlands	16,060	17,110	970	320	34,460
West Midlands	22,050	22,920	1,870	530	47,370
East of England	20,450	22,180	1,320	310	44,270
London	29,190	26,090	2,230	770	58,290
South East	29,200	29,630	2,360	650	61,830
South West	17,920	18,620	1,140	320	38,000
England	194,960	196,680	14,330	4,200	410,170
Wales	13,280	12,800	580	190	26,850
England and Wales	208,240	209,480	14,910	4,390	437,020

Source: DfES annual 618G survey and National Assembly for Wales stats3 survey.

1. Part-time teachers have been converted to an estimate of their full-time equivalency and added to full-time numbers.
2. Excludes occasional teachers.
3. Teachers whose service is divided between primary and secondary schools have been apportioned pro-rata to the nursery/primary or secondary phase.

TEACHERS IN SERVICE
Teacher numbers in the maintained schools sector: type of contract by LEA and Government Office region, 2001

ENGLAND AND WALES

	Qualified regular[1] full-time & secondments	Qualified regular[1] part-time FTE	Occasional teachers		Teachers without QTS[2]	Total FTE
			Agency	Other		
Darlington	740	30	30	20	10	830
Hartlepool	810	30	10	20	-	870
Middlesbrough	1,200	60	30	30	10	1,330
Redcar and Cleveland	1,210	60	10	30	10	1,320
Stockton on Tees	1,620	100	10	120	20	1,870
Durham	4,060	180	70	200	-	4,510
Northumberland	2,350	270	-	190	-	2,810
Gateshead	1,560	90	60	70	20	1,800
Newcastle upon Tyne	2,060	120	100	20	10	2,300
North Tyneside	1,680	130	70	30	10	1,920
South Tyneside	1,370	60	20	50	10	1,510
Sunderland	2,560	90	-	80	10	2,750
North East	**21,220**	**1,220**	**430**	**860**	**110**	**23,830**
Blackburn with Darwen	1,210	80	30	50	20	1,390
Blackpool	1,020	60	30	80	20	1,200
Halton	1,090	50	20	40	-	1,200
Warrington	1,560	100	10	50	20	1,740
Cheshire	5,090	480	40	140	30	5,780
Cumbria	3,680	470	10	160	30	4,360
Bolton	2,360	130	40	100	20	2,640
Bury	1,390	80	10	90	10	1,580
Manchester	3,510	170	120	130	100	4,040
Oldham	2,140	130	-	30	10	2,310
Rochdale	1,760	100	50	90	10	2,000
Salford	1,860	50	50	60	10	2,020
Stockport	2,170	160	30	90	-	2,450
Tameside	1,820	90	30	50	20	2,020
Trafford	1,770	130	20	80	-	2,000
Wigan	2,480	100	50	120	-	2,760
Lancashire	8,890	770	-	330	50	10,050
Knowsley	1,460	60	20	20	10	1,570
Liverpool	4,130	180	30	100	20	4,450
St Helens	1,500	70	-	60	-	1,630
Sefton	2,440	150	-	150	20	2,760
Wirral	2,830	180	70	100	10	3,190
North West	**56,170**	**3,800**	**660**	**2,090**	**420**	**63,120**

17 TEACHERS IN SERVICE

Teacher numbers in the maintained schools sector: type of contract by LEA and Government Office region, 2001

ENGLAND AND WALES

	Qualified regular[1] full-time & secondments	Qualified regular[1] part-time FTE	Occasional teachers		Teachers without QTS[2]	Total FTE
			Agency	Other		
East Riding of Yorkshire	2,310	210	40	100	20	2,670
City of Kingston Upon Hull	1,960	110	110	80	30	2,290
North East Lincolnshire	1,270	70	10	70	20	1,440
North Lincolnshire	1,230	90	20	60	20	1,410
York	1,190	180	30	70	10	1,480
North Yorkshire	4,370	520	40	230	40	5,200
Barnsley	1,570	60	40	100	-	1,780
Doncaster	2,520	160	20	80	20	2,790
Rotherham	2,340	140	40	100	20	2,640
Sheffield	3,660	470	-	210	50	4,400
Bradford	4,080	300	-	310	30	4,710
Calderdale	1,690	130	20	60	10	1,920
Kirklees	3,080	270	20	120	20	3,500
Leeds	5,620	400	110	130	10	6,280
Wakefield	2,580	90	30	110	20	2,840
Yorkshire and the Humber	**39,470**	**3,220**	**520**	**1,800**	**340**	**45,350**
Derby	1,780	160	-	-	30	1,980
Leicester	2,350	360	110	40	50	2,900
Nottingham	1,930	160	70	60	20	2,230
Rutland	220	30	-	30	-	270
Derbyshire	5,170	570	100	160	20	6,020
Leicestershire	4,390	570	50	130	60	5,200
Lincolnshire	4,850	410	-	220	40	5,520
Northamptonshire	4,870	410	10	190	60	5,520
Nottinghamshire	5,440	520	-	280	-	6,240
East Midlands	**30,980**	**3,190**	**340**	**1,100**	**290**	**35,900**
Herefordshire	1,160	140	-	60	-	1,360
Stoke on Trent	1,800	100	50	70	20	2,040
Telford and Wrekin	1,280	120	20	70	-	1,500
Shropshire	1,880	200	10	100	30	2,210
Staffordshire	6,290	480	60	250	30	7,120
Warwickshire	3,640	450	20	100	60	4,280
Birmingham	9,470	660	290	-	90	10,520
Coventry	2,560	250	20	90	50	2,980
Dudley	2,580	150	30	90	40	2,900
Sandwell	2,450	160	30	60	10	2,720
Solihull	1,860	180	30	50	20	2,130
Walsall	2,400	140	10	80	20	2,650
Wolverhampton	2,090	180	40	110	20	2,440
Worcestershire	3,830	430	20	130	10	4,430
West Midlands	**43,300**	**3,650**	**650**	**1,260**	**420**	**49,270**

TEACHERS IN SERVICE

17 Teacher numbers in the maintained schools sector: type of contract by LEA and Government Office region, 2001

ENGLAND AND WALES

	Qualified regular[1] full-time & secondments	Qualified regular[1] part-time FTE	Occasional teachers		Teachers without QTS[2]	Total FTE
			Agency	Other		
Luton	1,490	110	-	420	60	2,080
Peterborough	1,380	120	90	-	20	1,600
Southend on Sea	1,230	140	10	50	40	1,470
Thurrock	1,020	70	20	30	90	1,230
Bedfordshire	2,910	320	30	100	30	3,380
Cambridgeshire	3,500	450	30	60	90	4,120
Essex	9,490	840	180	300	190	10,990
Hertfordshire	7,950	1,030	40	80	190	9,290
Norfolk	5,100	550	-	220	100	6,270
Suffolk	4,850	550	-	240	90	5,740
East of England	**39,220**	**4,170**	**410**	**1,490**	**880**	**46,160**
Camden	1,180	190	60	10	70	1,500
City of London	10	-	-	-	-	20
Hackney	1,280	110	210	20	90	1,710
Hammersmith and Fulham	850	90	200	30	70	1,230
Haringey	1,710	110	70	30	30	1,950
Islington	1,130	110	110	10	50	1,420
Kensington and Chelsea	570	60	30	30	30	720
Lambeth	1,410	150	50	10	20	1,630
Lewisham	1,700	240	90	10	30	2,070
Newham	2,250	100	210	20	80	2,650
Southwark	1,720	140	100	20	110	2,090
Tower Hamlets	1,850	180	210	20	150	2,400
Wandsworth	1,480	190	50	10	70	1,790
City of Westminster	1,050	90	60	20	120	1,330
Barking and Dagenham	1,380	50	90	20	50	1,590
Barnet	2,280	370	70	30	90	2,840
Bexley	1,830	160	60	50	40	2,130
Brent	1,880	160	80	30	70	2,210
Bromley	2,220	270	40	70	60	2,660
Croydon	2,440	350	130	70	40	3,020
Ealing	1,960	160	80	20	100	2,320
Enfield	2,410	180	90	50	70	2,810
Greenwich	1,790	200	60	40	40	2,130
Harrow	1,280	170	60	60	40	1,610
Havering	1,710	160	40	50	70	2,040
Hillingdon	1,940	170	70	20	70	2,270
Hounslow	1,760	150	30	20	110	2,070
Kingston upon Thames	930	120	30	30	20	1,130
Merton	1,040	120	50	-	50	1,270
Redbridge	2,070	190	40	30	120	2,440
Richmond upon Thames	850	180	70	30	10	1,140
Sutton	1,360	140	30	10	20	1,570
Waltham Forest	1,740	130	-	40	70	1,980
London	**51,050**	**5,200**	**2,550**	**890**	**2,040**	**61,730**

17 TEACHERS IN SERVICE

Teacher numbers in the maintained schools sector: type of contract by LEA and Government Office region, 2001

ENGLAND AND WALES

	Qualified regular[1] full-time & secondments	Qualified regular[1] part-time FTE	Occasional teachers		Teachers without QTS[2]	Total FTE
			Agency	Other		
Bracknell Forest	670	80	20	10	10	790
Brighton and Hove	1,510	200	20	40	10	1,780
Isle of Wight	990	100	-	60	10	1,160
Medway	1,950	170	30	100	60	2,320
Milton Keynes	1,600	140	20	60	20	1,840
Portsmouth	1,350	100	30	50	30	1,550
Reading	890	100	30	30	10	1,050
Slough	940	110	40	30	50	1,150
Southampton	1,510	100	50	50	30	1,740
West Berkshire	1,190	130	-	30	10	1,360
Windsor and Maidenhead	870	110	20	-	10	1,010
Wokingham	1,130	140	-	30	10	1,310
Buckinghamshire	3,380	450	40	80	80	4,020
East Sussex	3,150	400	30	120	60	3,760
Hampshire	8,030	870	80	440	70	9,490
Kent	9,950	1,160	120	350	210	11,780
Oxfordshire	4,110	590	-	130	90	4,920
Surrey	6,370	820	90	170	110	7,560
West Sussex	5,000	570	40	170	30	5,820
South East	**54,580**	**6,350**	**650**	**1,930**	**910**	**64,410**
Bath and North East Somerset	1,240	150	10	40	-	1,450
Bournemouth	990	110	20	50	10	1,190
City of Bristol	2,580	200	80	70	10	2,940
North Somerset	1,280	130	-	70	10	1,490
Plymouth	2,030	180	-	170	10	2,380
Poole	940	90	10	20	-	1,060
South Gloucestershire	1,880	240	40	90	-	2,250
Swindon	1,340	90	30	20	10	1,500
Torbay	870	100	10	40	-	1,030
Cornwall	3,420	350	-	250	30	4,050
Isles of Scilly	20	-	-	-	-	20
Devon	4,380	610	270	-	30	5,300
Dorset	2,550	300	-	100	30	2,980
Gloucestershire	4,140	520	20	110	20	4,810
Somerset	3,360	370	30	300	40	4,100
Wiltshire	2,900	420	20	100	20	3,460
South West	**33,920**	**3,860**	**550**	**1,440**	**230**	**39,990**
England	**369,880**	**34,660**	**6,750**	**12,840**	**5,620**	**429,760**

17 TEACHERS IN SERVICE

Teacher numbers in the maintained schools sector: type of contract by LEA and Government Office region, 2001

ENGLAND AND WALES

	Qualified regular[1] full-time & secondments	Qualified regular[1] part-time FTE	Occasional teachers		Teachers without QTS[2]	Total FTE
			Agency	Other		
Isle of Anglesey	570	30	60	-	-	650
Gwynedd	1,000	80	80	-	-	1,160
Conwy	830	110	20	-	-	960
Denbighshire	770	10	60	-	-	840
Flintshire	1,220	100	40	-	-	1,350
Wrexham	880	80	140	-	-	1,110
Powys	1,100	110	130	-	10	1,340
Ceredigion	600	50	30	-	-	690
Pembrokeshire	1,050	80	120	-	-	1,260
Carmarthenshire	1,550	120	150	-	-	1,820
Swansea	1,890	110	-	-	-	2,000
Neath Port Talbot	1,270	60	-	-	-	1,340
Bridgend	1,230	20	50	-	10	1,300
Vale of Glamorgan	950	60	70	-	-	1,080
Rhondda Cynon Taff	2,270	50	10	-	-	2,330
Merthyr Tydfil	600	30	30	-	-	650
Caerphilly	1,520	60	50	-	10	1,650
Blaenau Gwent	640	60	0	-	-	700
Torfaen	710	40	60	-	-	810
Monmouthshire	630	60	30	-	-	710
Newport	1,320	70	90	-	-	1,480
Cardiff	2,610	210	70	-	-	2,890
Wales	**25,210**	**1,590**	**1,280**	**-**	**50**	**28,130**
England and Wales	**395,090**	**36,250**	**8,030**	**12,840**	**5,680**	**457,890**

Source: DfES annual 618G survey and National Assembly for Wales annual stats3 survey.

1. Includes regular supply teachers.
2. Teachers without Qualified Teacher Status.

18 TEACHERS IN SERVICE
Teacher numbers in the maintained schools sector: type of service by phase, January 2001

ENGLAND AND WALES

	England						Wales
	Qualified regular[1] full-time[2]	Qualified regular[1] part-time (fte)	Regular teachers without QTS[3]	Total regular	Occasional teachers	Total England	
Nursery and primary	171,330	16,630	2,020	189,970	11,810	201,780	13,610
Secondary	175,800	13,390	2,510	191,700	6,410	198,110	12,880
Miscellaneous primary and secondary[4]	6,780	2,450	740	9,970	290	10,260	820
Special[5]	12,700	1,320	300	14,330	820	15,150	620
Not in schools[5]	3,280	870	50	4,200	260	4,460	200
Total	369,880	34,660	5,620	410,170	19,590	429,760	28,130

Source: DfES annual 618G survey and National Assembly for Wales stats3 survey.

1. Includes regular supply teachers.
2. Includes teachers seconded for one term or more.
3. Teachers without Qualified Teacher Status (QTS), including instructors and those on routes to QTS.
4. Teachers whose service is divided between primary and secondary, peripatetic and advisory teachers and teachers in miscellaneous primary and secondary establishments.
5. Excluding non-maintained special schools.
6. Includes those teaching in pupil referral units and those employed by local education authorities but not teaching in schools or primary and secondary establishments, e.g. home tuition services.

19 TEACHERS IN SERVICE
Part-time qualified teachers in the maintained schools sector: 1985 to 2001

ENGLAND AND WALES

	Part-time teachers (thousands)		
	Number	Full-time equivalent (FTE)	FTE as % of total teaching force
1985[1]	35.8	16.1	3.6
1990[1]	52.0	24.0	5.5
1991[1]	54.1	25.3	5.8
1992[1]	57.2	27.0	6.2
1993[1]	58.3	27.7	6.3
1994	59.7	28.0	6.5
1995	61.9	29.3	6.8
1996	63.8	30.2	6.9
England only			
1996	62.5	29.7	7.2
1997	63.1	30.0	7.3
1998	64.2	30.7	7.5
1999	65.7	32.0	7.7
2000	68.0	33.3	7.9
2001	70.1	34.7	8.1
Of which:			
Nursery and primary[2]	37.7	17.9	8.6
Secondary[2]	28.0	14.6	7.2
Special and not in schools[3]	4.5	2.2	11.2

Source: DfES annual 618G survey and National Assembly for Wales stats3 survey.

1. Sixth form colleges are included to 1993.
2. Teachers whose service is divided between primary and secondary schools, peripatetic and advisory teachers and teachers in miscellaneous primary and secondary establishments are apportioned to nursery and primary or secondary schools.
3. Includes pupil referal units and those employed by local education authorities but not teaching in schools or primary and secondary establishments, e.g. home tuition services.

20

TEACHERS IN SERVICE
FTE teacher numbers in the maintained schools sector: 1996 to 2001 by country and sector

ENGLAND AND WALES

	1996	1997	1998	1999	2000	2001
England						
Nursery, primary and secondary	393,330	393,800	391,970	396,280	402,140	410,150
Special and education not in schools[1]	19,050	18,980	18,830	19,000	19,160	19,610
Total	412,390	412,790	410,800	415,280	421,290	429,760
Wales						
Nursery, primary and secondary	26,970	26,960	26,410	27,240	27,100	27,310
Special and education not in schools[1]	740	830	760	750	780	820
Total	27,710	27,790	27,170	27,990	27,880	28,130
England and Wales						
Nursery, primary and secondary	420,300	420,760	418,380	423,520	429,230	437,460
Special and education not in schools[1]	19,790	19,820	19,590	19,750	19,940	20,430
Total	440,100	440,580	437,970	443,270	449,170	457,890

Source: DfES annual 618G survey and National Assembly for Wales stats3 survey.

1. Includes pupil referal units and those employed by local education authorities but not teaching in schools or primary and secondary establishments, e.g. home tuition services. Excludes non-maintained special schools.

TEACHERS IN SERVICE
Full-time regular qualified teachers in the maintained schools sector: 1996-2000 by phase, grade and sex

ENGLAND

	1996		1997		1998[1]		1999[1]		2000[1]	
	Numbers (000s)	%	Numbers (000s)	%	Numbers (000s)	%	Numbers (000s)	%	Numbers (000s)	%
Nursery and primary										
Heads										
Men	8.9	46.1	8.4	44.3	8.0	42.2	7.6	41.0	7.5	40.2
Women	10.4	53.9	10.6	55.7	10.9	57.8	10.9	59.0	11.1	59.8
All teachers	19.3	100	19.0	100	18.9	100	18.5	100	18.6	100
Deputy heads										
Men	4.7	29.4	4.4	28.5	4.0	27.2	4.0	27.0	3.7	26.0
Women	11.2	70.6	11.0	71.5	10.8	72.8	10.8	73.0	10.5	74.0
All teachers	15.9	100	15.3	100	14.9	100	14.8	100	14.2	100
Classroom and others[2]										
Men	15.9	11.8	15.8	11.7	15.8	11.8	16.1	11.9	16.2	11.9
Women	118.5	88.2	119.0	88.3	118.4	88.2	119.4	88.1	120.1	88.1
All teachers	134.4	100	134.8	100	134.2	100	135.5	100	136.3	100
All teachers										
Men	29.4	17.3	28.6	16.9	27.8	16.6	27.7	16.4	27.4	16.2
Women	140.1	82.7	140.6	83.1	140.1	83.4	141.2	83.6	141.7	83.8
All teachers	169.5	100	169.2	100	167.9	100	168.8	100	169.1	100
Secondary										
Heads										
Men	3.1	75.2	3.0	74.3	3.0	72.3	2.9	71.4	2.8	70.7
Women	1.0	24.8	1.1	25.7	1.1	27.7	1.2	28.6	1.2	29.3
All teachers	4.1	100	4.1	100	4.1	100	4.1	100	4.0	100
Deputy heads										
Men	4.6	65.3	4.3	64.9	4.2	64.6	4.1	63.9	4.0	63.4
Women	2.5	34.7	2.3	35.1	2.3	35.4	2.3	36.1	2.3	36.6
All teachers	7.1	100	6.7	100	6.5	100	6.4	100	6.4	100
Classroom and others[2]										
Men	77.8	47.1	76.8	46.4	75.5	45.8	75.5	45.4	75.3	45.0
Women	87.4	52.9	88.7	53.6	89.3	54.2	90.8	54.6	92.2	55.0
All teachers	165.1	100	165.5	100	164.8	100	166.4	100	167.6	100
All teachers										
Men	85.5	48.5	84.2	47.8	82.6	47.1	82.6	46.7	82.2	46.2
Women	90.8	51.5	92.1	52.2	92.7	52.9	94.3	53.3	95.7	53.8
All teachers	176.3	100	176.2	100	175.3	100	176.8	100	177.9	100

21 TEACHERS IN SERVICE
Full-time regular qualified teachers in the maintained schools sector: 1996-2000 by phase, grade and sex

ENGLAND

	1996		1997		1998[1]		1999[1]		2000[1]	
	Numbers (000s)	%	Numbers (000s)	%	Numbers (000s)	%	Numbers (000s)	%	Numbers (000s)	%
Special and PRU										
Heads										
Men	0.8	60.7	0.7	58.7	0.7	57.1	0.7	55.9	0.7	54.1
Women	0.5	39.3	0.5	41.3	0.5	42.9	0.5	44.1	0.6	45.9
All teachers	1.2	100	1.2	100	1.2	100	1.2	100	1.2	100
Deputy heads										
Men	0.6	48.6	0.6	46.0	0.5	45.1	0.5	43.6	0.5	42.4
Women	0.6	51.4	0.7	54.0	0.6	54.9	0.6	56.4	0.6	57.6
All teachers	1.2	100	1.2	100	1.2	100	1.1	100	1.1	100
Classroom and others[2]										
Men	3.6	28.9	3.5	29.0	3.5	29.2	3.5	29.2	3.4	29.2
Women	8.8	71.1	8.6	71.0	8.4	70.8	8.4	70.8	8.3	70.8
All teachers	12.4	100	12.1	100	11.9	100	11.8	100	11.8	100
All teachers										
Men	4.9	33.2	4.8	32.9	4.7	32.9	4.6	32.7	4.6	32.4
Women	9.9	66.8	9.8	67.1	9.6	67.1	9.6	67.3	9.6	67.6
All teachers	14.8	100	14.6	100	14.3	100	14.2	100	14.1	100
Total										
Heads										
Men	12.7	51.7	12.2	50.0	11.7	48.1	11.2	47.0	11.0	46.0
Women	11.9	48.3	12.2	50.0	12.6	51.9	12.6	53.0	12.9	54.0
All teachers	24.6	100	24.3	100	24.2	100	23.8	100	23.9	100
Deputy heads										
Men	9.9	40.9	9.2	39.8	8.7	38.9	8.6	38.4	8.2	37.8
Women	14.3	59.1	13.9	60.2	13.8	61.1	13.8	61.6	13.5	62.2
All teachers	24.2	100	23.2	100	22.5	100	22.4	100	21.7	100
Classroom and others[2]										
Men	97.2	31.2	96.1	30.8	94.8	30.5	95.1	30.3	95.0	30.1
Women	214.7	68.8	216.3	69.2	216.1	69.5	218.6	69.7	220.7	69.9
All teachers	311.9	100	312.5	100	310.9	100	313.7	100	315.6	100
All teachers										
Men	119.8	33.2	117.6	32.7	115.1	32.2	114.9	31.9	114.2	31.6
Women	240.9	66.8	242.4	67.3	242.5	67.8	245.0	68.1	247.0	68.4
All teachers	360.7	100	360.0	100	357.6	100	359.9	100	361.2	100

Source: Database of Teacher Records.

1. Provisional estimates.
2. Includes teachers whose grade is unknown.

TEACHERS IN SERVICE

22

Full-time regular qualified teachers in the maintained schools sector 1985 to 2000 by sex and graduate status

ENGLAND

	1985[1]	1990[1]	1995	1996	1997	1998[2]	1999[2]	2000[2]
Men								
Graduates	89.3	84.3	82.6	83.4	84.2	84.8	86.0	86.8
Graduate equivalents	4.8	3.7	2.6	2.5	2.3	2.3	2.2	2.2
Other[3]	66.3	49.9	36.7	34.0	31.0	28.1	26.7	25.2
Total men	160.4	138.0	121.9	119.8	117.6	115.1	114.9	114.2
Women								
Graduates	89.8	105.4	129.9	136.7	144.8	151.7	157.9	164.2
Graduate equivalents	3.6	3.2	2.5	2.6	2.6	2.6	2.7	2.7
Other[3]	144.5	129.3	107.4	101.5	95.0	88.1	84.4	80.1
Total women	237.9	237.9	239.8	240.9	242.4	242.5	245.0	247.0
Men and women								
Graduates	179.1	189.7	212.5	220.1	229.1	236.5	243.9	251.0
Graduate equivalents	8.4	7.0	5.1	5.1	4.9	4.9	4.9	4.8
Other[3]	210.8	179.3	144.1	135.4	126.0	116.2	111.1	105.3
Total	398.3	375.9	361.7	360.7	360.0	357.6	359.9	361.2

Source: Database of Teacher Records.

1. 1985 and 1990 include sixth form colleges.

2. Provisional data.

3. Includes head teachers and deputy heads with graduate equivalent qualifications as they cannot be identified separately. May also include some teachers who achieved graduate or equivalent qualifications after achieving Qualified Teacher Status (QTS), and whose graduate qualifications have not been recorded.

TEACHERS IN SERVICE

23

Full-time regular qualified teachers in the maintained schools sector: 1985 to 2000 by sex and type of school

ENGLAND

	1985	1990	1995	1996	1997	1998[1]	1999[1]	2000[1]
Men								
Nursery	10	20	40	50	40	40	40	40
Primary[2]								
Grant-maintained	.	.	780	900	960	1,080	1,080	.
LEA Maintained	34,680	31,890	28,940	28,450	27,590	26,690	26,550	.
All primary schools	34,680	31,890	29,720	29,350	28,540	27,770	27,630	27,340
Secondary[3]								
Grant-maintained	.	480	16,010	16,400	16,880	16,930	16,990	.
LEA Maintained	119,420	99,430	70,650	68,480	66,720	65,130	65,040	.
All secondary schools	119,420	99,900	86,660	84,880	83,600	82,070	82,030	81,690
Divided service[4]	580	860	580	610	580	540	520	500
Special	5,720	5,300	4,760	4,730	4,590	4,450	4,360	4,260
Pupil Referral Units	.	.	140	200	210	270	280	320
Total men	160,400	137,970	121,910	119,820	117,560	115,130	114,870	114,160
Women								
Nursery	1,530	1,480	1,380	1,360	1,340	1,300	1,270	1,260
Primary[2]								
Grant-maintained	.	.	3,500	3,920	4,240	4,510	4,610	.
LEA Maintained	123,320	133,210	134,580	134,830	135,000	134,320	135,280	.
All primary schools	123,320	133,210	138,070	138,760	139,240	138,830	139,890	140,470
Secondary[3]								
Grant-maintained	.	290	15,240	16,090	16,810	17,460	17,740	.
LEA Maintained	101,060	91,040	74,040	73,480	74,070	74,200	75,460	.
All secondary schools	101,060	91,330	89,280	89,560	90,880	91,660	93,200	94,660
Divided service[4]	1,090	1,420	1,270	1,290	1,180	1,080	1,090	1,060
Special	10,900	10,480	9,600	9,560	9,380	9,160	9,100	9,030
Pupil Referral Units	.	.	210	360	400	440	470	520
Total women	237,900	237,910	239,810	240,870	242,420	242,460	245,020	247,000
Men and Women								
Nursery	1,540	1,500	1,420	1,410	1,380	1,340	1,320	1,300
Primary[2]								
Grant-maintained	.	.	4,280	4,820	5,200	5,590	5,690	.
LEA Maintained	158,000	165,100	163,510	163,280	162,590	161,010	161,830	.
All primary schools	158,000	165,100	167,790	168,100	167,780	166,600	167,520	167,810
Secondary[3]								
Grant-maintained	.	770	31,250	32,490	33,690	34,390	34,730	.
LEA Maintained	220,480	190,470	144,690	141,960	140,790	139,330	140,510	.
All secondary schools	220,480	191,230	175,940	174,450	174,480	173,730	175,230	176,350
Divided service[4]	1,660	2,280	1,860	1,890	1,760	1,620	1,610	1,570
Special	16,620	15,770	14,360	14,290	13,960	13,610	13,460	13,300
Pupil Referral Units	.	.	350	560	620	700	750	840
Total	398,300	375,880	361,720	360,690	359,980	357,590	359,890	361,160

Source: Database of Teacher Records

1. Provisional data
2. Including middle schools deemed primary.
3. Including middle schools deemed secondary. Includes sixth form colleges in 1985 and 1990.
4. Teachers whose full-time service was divided between primary and secondary schools.

24

TEACHERS IN SERVICE
Graduate full-time qualified regular teachers in the maintained schools sector: first degree subject by sex and class of degree, March 2000[1]

ENGLAND

	Degree subject group					
	Education	Medicine	Technology	Agriculture	Mathematics[2]	Other science
Men						
Maintained nursery, primary and secondary						
1st class honours	300	10	100	10	360	650
2nd class honours	10,050	160	1,700	250	2,860	10,030
Other degrees	7,750	60	1,430	70	2,560	5,950
Total	18,100	230	3,230	330	5,780	16,630
Special and PRU						
1st class honours	20	-	-	-	-	10
2nd class honours	480	-	20	10	40	220
Other degrees	460	-	30	-	50	180
Total	960	10	60	10	90	400
Total						
1st class honours	310	10	100	10	360	660
2nd class honours	10,530	160	1,720	260	2,900	10,240
Other degrees	8,210	70	1,460	70	2,610	6,130
Total	19,050	240	3,290	340	5,870	17,040
Women						
Maintained nursery, primary and secondary						
1st class honours	780	20	50	20	550	840
2nd class honours	20,920	520	600	340	5,170	13,240
Other degrees	13,990	130	310	70	2,030	3,300
Total	35,690	680	960	420	7,750	17,380
Special and PRU						
1st class honours	30	-	-	-	-	10
2nd class honours	950	20	20	10	70	280
Other degrees	960	10	10	-	40	110
Total	1,940	30	30	10	120	400
Total						
1st class honours	810	20	50	20	550	850
2nd class honours	21,860	540	620	350	5,250	13,520
Other degrees	14,960	140	320	70	2,060	3,400
Total	37,630	710	990	440	7,870	17,770
Men and Women						
Maintained nursery, primary and secondary	53,790	900	4,190	750	13,530	34,010
Special and PRU	2,900	40	80	30	210	800
Total	56,680	940	4,270	780	13,730	34,810

24 **TEACHERS IN SERVICE**

Graduate full-time qualified regular teachers in the maintained schools sector: first degree subject by sex and class of degree, March 2000[1]

ENGLAND

	Degree subject group					
	Education	Medicine	Technology	Agriculture	Mathematics[2]	Other science
Men						
Maintained nursery, primary and secondary						
1st class honours	200	400	240	270	20	2,550
2nd class honours	10,250	7,640	7,390	3,610	590	54,510
Other degrees	2,180	1,450	4,200	880	470	27,000
Total	12,630	9,480	11,830	4,760	1,070	84,060
Special and PRU						
1st class honours	10	10	-	10	-	50
2nd class honours	330	150	170	120	20	1,560
Other degrees	100	50	200	50	30	1,150
Total	430	210	370	180	40	2,760
Total						
1st class honours	210	400	240	280	20	2,600
2nd class honours	10,580	7,790	7,560	3,730	600	56,060
Other degrees	2,280	1,500	4,400	930	490	28,160
Total	13,060	9,690	12,210	4,930	1,110	86,820
Women						
Maintained nursery, primary and secondary						
1st class honours	540	990	450	520	80	4,850
2nd class honours	20,150	29,350	16,560	12,000	1,460	120,310
Other degrees	2,830	4,790	4,140	1,720	900	34,210
Total	23,520	35,140	21,150	14,240	2,440	159,360
Special and PRU						
1st class honours	20	10	10	10	-	90
2nd class honours	580	530	330	300	40	3,110
Other degrees	120	120	180	60	30	1,640
Total	710	650	520	370	70	4,840
Total						
1st class honours	560	1,000	450	530	80	4,930
2nd class honours	20,730	29,880	16,890	12,290	1,500	123,420
Other degrees	2,950	4,910	4,320	1,790	930	35,850
Total	24,230	35,790	21,670	14,610	2,510	164,200
Men and Women						
Maintained nursery, primary and secondary	36,150	44,620	32,980	19,000	3,510	243,420
Special and PRU	1,140	860	890	540	110	7,600
Total	37,300	45,480	33,870	19,540	3,620	251,020

Source: Database of Teacher Records.

1. Provisional data.
2. Mathematics includes statistics and computer studies.

25 TEACHERS IN SERVICE

Full-time regular qualified teachers at March 2000: grade and sex by phase and length of experience[1]

ENGLAND

(thousands)

	Head			Deputy Head			Classroom		
	Men	Women	Total	Men	Women	Total	Men	Women	Total
Nursery and primary									
0 - 4 years	-	-	-	-	0.1	0.1	5.8	39.9	45.7
5 - 9 years	0.1	0.3	0.4	0.5	1.3	1.8	3.4	23.2	26.6
10 - 14 years	0.4	1.0	1.5	0.6	2.0	2.7	1.6	14.9	16.4
15 - 19 years	0.6	2.0	2.6	0.4	2.3	2.6	0.8	15.7	16.5
20+ years	6.3	7.8	14.1	2.2	4.8	7.0	4.5	25.8	30.2
Total	7.5	11.1	18.6	3.7	10.5	14.2	16.1	119.4	135.5
Secondary									
0 - 4 years	-	-	-	-	-	-	16.1	25.6	41.7
5 - 9 years	-	-	-	-	-	0.1	11.2	14.7	25.9
10 - 14 years	-	-	0.1	0.2	0.2	0.4	7.4	11.4	18.8
15 - 19 years	0.2	0.2	0.4	0.5	0.5	1.1	8.8	14.8	23.7
20+ years	2.6	0.9	3.5	3.2	1.6	4.8	31.4	25.1	56.5
Total	2.8	1.2	4.0	4.0	2.3	6.4	75.0	91.7	166.6
Special and PRU									
0 - 4 years	-	-	-	-	-	-	0.5	1.1	1.6
5 - 9 years	-	-	-	-	-	0.1	0.5	1.3	1.7
10 - 14 years	-	-	0.1	-	0.1	0.1	0.4	1.4	1.9
15 - 19 years	0.1	0.1	0.2	0.1	0.2	0.3	0.6	1.8	2.4
20+ years	0.5	0.4	0.9	0.3	0.3	0.7	1.4	2.7	4.1
Total	0.7	0.6	1.2	0.5	0.6	1.1	3.4	8.3	11.7
Total									
0 - 4 years	-	-	-	0.1	0.1	0.1	22.5	66.6	89.1
5 - 9 years	0.1	0.3	0.4	0.5	1 4	1.9	15.0	39.2	54.2
10 - 14 years	0.5	1.1	1.7	0.9	2.3	3.2	9.4	27.7	37.1
15 - 19 years	0.9	2.3	3.2	1.0	2.9	3.9	10.2	32.3	42.6
20+ years	9.4	9.1	18.6	5.7	6.7	12.4	37.3	53.5	90.9
Total	11.0	12.9	23.9	8.2	13.5	21.7	94.5	219.4	313.8

25 TEACHERS IN SERVICE

Full-time regular qualified teachers at March 2000: grade and sex by phase and length of experience[1]

ENGLAND   (thousands)

| | Teachers in each length of service band | | | | | |
| | Grade not known | | | Total | | |
	Men	Women	Total	Men	Women	Total
Nursery and primary						
0 - 4 years	0.1	0.7	0.8	6.0	40.7	46.7
5 - 9 years	-	-	-	4.0	24.8	28.8
10 - 14 years	-	-	-	2.6	17.9	20.6
15 - 19 years	-	-	-	1.8	19.9	21.7
20 + years	-	-	-	13.0	38.4	51.4
Total	0.1	0.7	0.8	27.4	141.7	169.1
Secondary						
0 - 4 years	0.3	0.5	0.9	16.5	26.1	42.6
5 - 9 years	-	-	-	11.2	14.8	26.0
10 - 14 years	-	-	-	7.7	11.7	19.4
15 - 19 years	-	-	-	9.6	15.5	25.1
20 + years	-	-	-	37.2	27.6	64.8
Total	0.4	0.6	0.9	82.2	95.7	177.9
Special						
0 - 4 years	-	-	-	0.5	1.1	1.7
5 - 9 years	-	-	-	0.5	1.3	1.8
10 - 14 years	-	-	-	0.5	1.6	2.1
15 - 19 years	-	-	-	0.7	2.1	2.9
20 + years	-	-	-	2.3	3.4	5.7
Total	-	-	-	4.6	9.6	14.1
All sectors						
0 - 4 years	0.5	1.2	1.7	23.0	68.0	90.9
5 - 9 years	-	0.1	0.1	15.7	40.9	56.6
10 - 14 years	-	-	-	10.8	31.2	42.0
15 - 19 years	-	-	-	12.2	37.6	49.7
20 + years	-	-	-	52.5	69.4	121.9
Total	0.5	1.3	1.8	114.2	247.0	361.2

Source: Database of Teacher Records.

1. Provisional data

TEACHERS IN SERVICE

26 Full-time regular qualified teachers in the maintained schools sector by phase, grade, age and sex, March 2000[1]

ENGLAND

(thousands)

	Nursery and Primary				Secondary			
	Heads	Deputy heads	Classroom and others[3]	total	Heads	Deputy heads	Classroom and others[2]	total
Men								
Under 25	0.0	0.0	0.8	0.8	0.0	0.0	1.7	1.7
25-29	0.0	0.1	3.1	3.2	0.0	0.0	8.8	8.8
30-34	0.1	0.4	2.8	3.3	0.0	0.1	9.0	9.1
35-39	0.4	0.6	2.2	3.2	0.0	0.3	8.9	9.2
40-44	1.0	0.6	1.9	3.4	0.3	0.7	11.3	12.3
45-49	2.3	1.0	2.7	5.9	0.8	1.2	16.6	18.6
50-54	2.6	0.9	2.1	5.6	1.1	1.3	14.1	16.6
55-59	1.0	0.2	0.5	1.7	0.5	0.5	4.0	5.0
60 and over	0.1	0.0	0.1	0.2	0.1	0.1	0.7	0.9
All ages	7.5	3.7	16.2	27.4	2.8	4.0	75.3	82.2
Women								
Under 25	0.0	0.0	9.0	9.0	0.0	0.0	4.3	4.3
25-29	0.0	0.2	24.0	24.2	0.0	0.0	16.3	16.3
30-34	0.2	1.2	14.8	16.1	0.0	0.0	11.6	11.6
35-39	0.6	1.3	10.3	12.2	0.0	0.2	9.5	9.8
40-44	1.5	1.7	14.4	17.7	0.2	0.5	13.4	14.1
45-49	3.4	3.0	22.6	29.0	0.4	0.7	17.9	19.0
50-54	3.6	2.3	18.2	24.1	0.4	0.6	13.6	14.6
55-59	1.5	0.8	6.0	8.3	0.2	0.2	4.8	5.2
60 and over	0.2	0.1	0.7	1.1	0.0	0.0	0.7	0.8
All ages	11.1	10.5	120.1	141.7	1.2	2.3	92.2	95.7
Men and Women								
Under 25	0.0	0.0	9.9	9.9	0.0	0.0	6.1	6.1
25-29	0.0	0.2	27.2	27.4	0.0	0.0	25.1	25.1
30-34	0.3	1.6	17.5	19.4	0.0	0.1	20.6	20.7
35-39	1.0	1.9	12.5	15.3	0.1	0.5	18.5	19.0
40-44	2.5	2.3	16.3	21.1	0.5	1.2	24.7	26.4
45-49	5.7	4.0	25.3	35.0	1.2	1.9	34.5	37.5
50-54	6.3	3.2	20.3	29.7	1.5	1.9	27.8	31.1
55-59	2.5	1.0	6.6	10.1	0.7	0.7	8.9	10.3
60 and over	0.4	0.1	0.8	1.3	0.1	0.1	1.4	1.6
All ages	18.6	14.2	136.3	169.1	4.0	6.4	167.6	177.9

CONTINUED
TEACHERS IN SERVICE
Full-time regular qualified teachers in the maintained schools sector by phase, grade, age and sex, March 2000[1]

ENGLAND   (thousands)

	Special and PRU				Total			
	Heads	Deputy heads	Classroom and others[2]	total	Heads	Deputy heads	Classroom and others[2]	total
Men								
Under 25	0.0	0.0	0.0	0.0	0.0	0.0	2.6	2.6
25-29	0.0	0.0	0.2	0.2	0.0	0.1	12.1	12.2
30-34	0.0	0.0	0.3	0.3	0.1	0.5	12.1	12.7
35-39	0.0	0.0	0.4	0.5	0.5	0.9	11.5	12.9
40-44	0.1	0.1	0.7	0.9	1.4	1.3	13.8	16.5
45-49	0.2	0.2	1.0	1.4	3.3	2.3	20.2	25.9
50-54	0.2	0.1	0.7	1.0	3.9	2.3	16.9	23.2
55-59	0.1	0.0	0.2	0.3	1.6	0.7	4.8	7.1
60 and over	0.0	0.0	0.0	0.0	0.2	0.1	0.8	1.1
All ages	0.7	0.5	3.4	4.6	11.0	8.2	95.0	114.2
Women								
Under 25	0.0	0.0	0.1	0.1	0.0	0.0	13.4	13.4
25-29	0.0	0.0	0.6	0.6	0.0	0.2	40.9	41.1
30-34	0.0	0.0	0.7	0.7	0.2	1.2	27.1	28.5
35-39	0.0	0.1	0.8	0.9	0.7	1.6	20.6	22.9
40-44	0.1	0.1	1.5	1.7	1.8	2.4	29.3	33.5
45-49	0.2	0.2	2.2	2.6	4.0	3.9	42.7	50.6
50-54	0.2	0.2	1.8	2.1	4.2	3.1	33.5	40.8
55-59	0.1	0.1	0.7	0.8	1.8	1.0	11.5	14.4
60 and over	0.0	0.0	0.1	0.1	0.3	0.1	1.5	1.9
All ages	0.6	0.6	8.3	9.6	12.9	13.5	220.7	247.0
Men and Women								
Under 25	0.0	0.0	0.1	0.1	0.0	0.0	16.0	16.0
25-29	0.0	0.0	0.8	0.8	0.0	0.2	53.0	53.3
30-34	0.0	0.0	1.0	1.0	0.3	1.7	39.1	41.2
35-39	0.1	0.1	1.2	1.4	1.1	2.4	32.1	35.7
40-44	0.2	0.2	2.2	2.6	3.2	3.7	43.1	50.0
45-49	0.4	0.4	3.2	4.0	7.3	6.2	63.0	76.5
50-54	0.4	0.3	2.4	3.1	8.1	5.4	50.5	64.0
55-59	0.2	0.1	0.8	1.1	3.4	1.8	16.3	21.5
60 and over	0.0	0.0	0.1	0.1	0.5	0.2	2.3	3.0
All ages	1.2	1.1	11.8	14.1	23.9	21.7	315.6	361.2

Source: Database of Teacher Records.

1. Provisional data.
2. Includes grade unknown.

TEACHERS IN SERVICE

27

Full-time teachers in maintained secondary schools: age at November 1996 by subject of qualification[1]

ENGLAND

	Percentages					Total numbers (000s)
	Under 30	30-39	40-49	50 or over	Total	
Subject:						
Mathematics	15	22	43	20	100	27.1
English	16	23	44	17	100	31.6
Biology	16	24	44	15	100	11.3
Chemistry	14	20	42	23	100	10.7
Physics	11	21	44	24	100	10.4
General Science	20	25	39	16	100	15.5
Other Sciences	16	28	39	18	100	6.2
French	19	25	41	15	100	15.5
German	23	24	40	13	100	6.9
Spanish	28	26	34	12	100	2.5
Other Modern Languages	25	23	38	14	100	2.7
Design & Technology	13	25	43	19	100	11.1
Information Technology	18	23	47	12	100	4.9
Other Technology	18	27	37	18	100	4.4
Home Economics	7	22	49	22	100	6.8
Business Studies	24	26	34	16	100	4.3
Classics	9	22	32	38	100	1.4
History	16	23	43	18	100	19.2
Religious Education	17	24	40	20	100	8.6
Geography	16	21	49	14	100	15.6
Other Social Studies	14	23	48	15	100	11.3
Combined Arts/Humanities/Social Studies	15	23	43	19	100	4.2
Music	23	24	36	16	100	6.3
Drama	20	29	41	10	100	8.0
Art	12	23	45	20	100	10.8
Physical Education	19	27	43	11	100	22.0
Careers	3	12	55	30	100	0.9
Personal and Social Education	15	21	49	15	100	2.3
General Studies	12	23	46	20	100	2.2
General Primary Subjects	8	22	62	8	100	1.0
Other	10	21	48	21	100	21.5
Total[1]	16	24	43	17	100	307.2
Full-time teachers	17	24	43	17	100	170.1

Source: 1996/97 Secondary Schools Curriculum and Staffing Survey

1. Teachers are counted once against each subject in which they have a post A level qualification.

28 TEACHERS IN SERVICE
Full-time teachers in maintained secondary schools - highest level of qualification[1] by subject of qualification[2], at November 1996

ENGLAND

	Percentages						Total numbers (000s)
	Degree[3]	BEd	PGCE	Cert Ed	Other qual.	Total	
Mathematics	47	18	15	17	3	100	27.1
English	49	18	14	18	1	100	31.6
Biology	55	13	14	18	1	100	11.3
Chemistry	66	10	14	10	-	100	10.7
Physics	53	12	20	13	2	100	10.4
General Science	29	13	44	13	1	100	15.5
Other Sciences	66	10	12	10	2	100	6.2
French	59	12	16	10	2	100	15.5
German	64	11	18	4	3	100	6.9
Spanish	68	5	21	-	6	100	2.5
Other Modern Languages	68	5	18	4	5	100	2.7
Design & Technology	16	32	13	35	4	100	11.1
Information Technology	36	17	19	8	20	100	4.9
Other Technology	47	13	6	19	15	100	4.4
Home Economics	13	25	4	55	3	100	6.8
Business Studies	31	22	18	17	12	100	4.3
Classics	83	3	7	2	6	100	1.4
History	54	14	14	17	1	100	19.2
Religious Education	34	20	17	26	3	100	8.6
Geography	43	22	12	23	1	100	15.6
Other Social Studies	70	14	8	6	3	100	11.3
Combined Arts/Humanities/Social Studies	55	19	14	11	1	100	4.2
Music	49	16	9	23	2	100	6.3
Drama	27	19	25	25	4	100	8.0
Art	42	17	9	30	3	100	10.8
Physical Education	13	37	11	38	1	100	22.0
Careers Education	11	10	11	20	48	100	0.9
Personal and Social Education	24	17	22	20	16	100	2.3
General Studies	20	23	28	24	5	100	2.2
General Primary Subjects	14	9	48	21	8	100	1.0
Other	45	13	10	10	22	100	21.5
Total[2]	44	18	15	19	4	100	307.2

Source: 1996/97 Secondary Schools Curriculum and Staffing Survey.

1. Where a teacher has more than one post A level qualification in the same subject, the qualification level is determined by the highest level reading from left (Degree) to right (Other Qualifications). For example, teachers shown under PGCE have a PGCE but not a degree or BEd in the subject, while those with a PGCE and a degree are shown only under Degree.
2. Teachers are counted once against each subject in which they have a post A level qualification.
3. Includes higher degrees but excludes BEds.

TEACHERS IN SERVICE

29

Full-time teachers in maintained secondary schools teaching named subjects: highest level of qualification[1] in subjects taught[2] to years 7-13, at November 1996

ENGLAND

	Percentages							Total numbers (000s)
	Degree[3]	BEd	PGCE	Cert Ed	Other qual.	No qual	Total	
Mathematics	40	16	11	12	2	20	100	25.2
English	43	14	9	12	-	22	100	28.4
Biology[4]	63	11	15	5	-	6	100	5.1
Chemistry[4]	75	5	15	2	-	3	100	4.6
Physics[4]	62	8	21	3	-	6	100	4.4
General Science[4]	57	12	13	9	-	9	100	27.3
Other Sciences	23	-	4	2	-	71	100	1.6
French	50	10	13	7	2	18	100	16.2
German	47	8	14	2	2	27	100	8.1
Spanish	45	3	13	-	4	35	100	2.7
Other Modern Languages	22	2	3	-	1	73	100	1.3
Design & Technology[5]	13	18	6	20	1	42	100	18.6
Information Technology[5]	10	5	5	3	5	73	100	10.7
Combined Technology[5]	14	21	5	19	2	39	100	5.2
Home Economics	8	20	3	44	2	23	100	5.0
Business Studies	16	13	11	9	4	47	100	6.4
Classics	57	-	-	-	-	43	100	0.5
History	47	10	10	8	1	25	100	13.8
Religious Education	19	10	7	9	1	55	100	13.4
Geography	38	15	8	11	-	27	100	14.2
Other Social Studies	36	6	5	2	1	50	100	5.0
Combined Arts/Humanities/Social Studies	8	3	2	1	-	85	100	6.3
Music	49	13	8	15	2	13	100	5.6
Drama	16	10	9	11	2	53	100	8.9
Art	41	12	7	18	2	19	100	9.4
Physical Education	11	34	5	23	-	26	100	20.0
Careers Education	2	1	1	3	3	91	100	1.9
Personal and Social Education	1	-	-	-	-	98	100	74.2
General Studies	1	2	2	1	-	94	100	7.9
Other	.	.	.	.	.	.	.	27.8
Total[2,6]	27	10	7	9	1	46	100	379.7

Source: 1996/97 Secondary Schools Curriculum and Staffing Survey.

1. Where a teacher has more than one post A level qualification in the same subject, the qualification level is determined by the highest level reading from left (Degree) to right (Other Qualifications). For example, teachers shown under PGCE have a PGCE but not a degree or BEd in the subject, while those with a PGCE and a degree are shown only under Degree.
2. Teachers are counted once against each subject which they are teaching.
3. Includes higher degrees but excludes BEds.
4. "Teachers qualified in general science are treated as qualified to teach biology, chemistry, or physics. Teachers qualified in biology, chemistry or physics are treated as qualified to teach general science.
5. Teachers qualified in other technology are treated as qualified to teach design & technology or information technology. Teachers qualified in design and technology or information technology are treated as qualified to teach combined technology.
6. 'Other' not included in total percentages.

TEACHERS IN SERVICE

30

Full-time teachers in maintained secondary schools - Highest level of qualification[1] in subjects taught[2] to years 7-13 by percentage of periods taught in subject, at November 1996

ENGLAND

	Percentage of periods taught in subject							Tuition in subject as percentage of all tuition
	Degree[3]	BEd	PGCE	Cert Ed	Other qual.	No qual.	Total	
Mathematics	47	18	12	12	2	9	100	11.7
English	53	15	10	12	-	10	100	11.8
Biology[4]	67	9	13	5	-	5	100	1.0
Chemistry[4]	80	5	11	2	-	1	100	0.9
Physics[4]	67	7	20	3	-	3	100	0.8
Combined/General Science[4]	59	12	14	10	-	5	100	12.0
Other Sciences	28	-	5	3	-	64	100	0.3
French	55	11	13	8	2	10	100	6.1
German	55	9	15	3	1	17	100	2.3
Spanish	55	3	12	-	5	25	100	0.7
Other Modern Languages	29	2	3	-	3	63	100	0.3
Design and Technology[5]	14	22	7	24	1	31	100	7.4
Information Technology[5]	16	7	7	4	7	58	100	2.0
Combined Technology[5]	14	23	5	24	2	33	100	1.3
Home Economics	9	24	4	44	2	17	100	1.2
Business Studies	21	17	13	12	5	31	100	1.9
Classics	83	-	-	-	-	17	100	0.2
History	59	11	11	7	-	12	100	4.7
Religious Education	35	17	12	14	1	21	100	3.2
Geography	51	16	10	11	-	11	100	5.1
Other Social Studies	44	7	6	3	1	40	100	1.0
Combined Arts/Humanities/Social Studies	9	4	2	2	-	82	100	1.3
Music	56	15	9	15	2	3	100	2.5
Drama	25	15	9	15	4	32	100	2.0
Art	50	13	8	20	2	7	100	4.1
Physical Education	15	47	5	27	-	6	100	7.1
Careers Education	1	2	1	6	3	87	100	0.1
Personal and Social Education	1	1	-	1	1	96	100	3.1
General Studies	3	9	6	1	-	81	100	0.4
Other	.	.	.	.	.	.	.	3.4
Total[2,6]	42	16	10	13	1	18	100	100.0

Source : 1996/97 Secondary Schools Curriculum and Staffing Survey.

1. Where a teacher has more than one post A level qualification in the same subject, the qualification level is determined by the highest level reading from left (Degree) to right (Other Qualifications). For example, teachers shown under PGCE have a PGCE but not a degree on BEd in the subject, while those with a PGCE and a degree are shown only under Degree.
2. Teachers are counted once against each subject which they are teaching.
3. Includes higher degrees but excludes BEds.
4. Teachers qualified in general science are treated as qualified to teach biology, chemistry, or physics. Teachers qualified in biology, chemistry, or physics are treated as qualified to teach general science.
5. Teachers qualified in other technology are treated as qualified to teach design & technology or information technology. Teachers qualified in design and technology or information technology are treated as qualified to teach combined technology.
6. 'Other' not included in total percentages.

31 TEACHERS IN SERVICE

Advanced Skills Teachers[1] in the maintained schools sector January 2001 by phase and region

ENGLAND

	Nursery and primary	Secondary	Special	Total
North East	10	20	-	20
North West	20	40	-	60
Yorkshire and The Humber	10	20	-	40
East Midlands	10	40	-	50
West Midlands	20	40	-	50
East of England	20	70	10	100
London	20	70	10	90
South East	40	50	-	90
South West	20	40	-	60
England	160	380	20	560

Sources: DfES annual 618G survey and Westminster Education Consultants (WEC).

1. Data from the two sources were matched together, and discrepancies investigated, to produce complete information.

TEACHERS PAY

Full-time regular qualified teachers in the maintained schools sector March 2000 by spine point[1] and age[2]

ENGLAND AND WALES   i. Men

	Percentage of teachers in each age band							Total numbers (thousands)
	Classroom teachers' pay spine[1]				Deputy heads	Heads	Total	
	0 - 8.5	9	9.5 - 13.5	14 - 17				
Nursery & Primary								
Under 25	100.0	-	-	-	-	-	100	0.9
25-29	91.2	4.1	2.6	-	1.8	0.3	100	3.5
30-34	43.3	13.9	26.4	0.1	12.7	3.7	100	3.6
35-39	21.1	16.1	30.8	0.3	18.4	13.4	100	3.4
40-44	9.9	13.3	29.8	0.3	17.3	29.4	100	3.7
45-49	2.9	12.0	28.7	0.5	17.1	38.8	100	6.4
50-54	1.2	10.4	24.4	0.7	15.5	47.8	100	6.0
55-59	0.2	9.2	20.5	0.9	12.3	56.9	100	1.9
60 and over	-	12.0	24.9	0.4	10.8	51.8	100	0.3
All ages	23.3	11.1	23.5	0.4	13.8	28.0	100	29.6
Secondary								
Under 25	100.0	-	-	-	-	-	100	1.8
25-29	87.0	5.6	7.3	0.1	-	-	100	9.4
30-34	41.0	13.9	43.0	1.5	0.6	-	100	9.7
35-39	16.7	13.6	62.1	4.3	2.9	0.5	100	9.8
40-44	6.3	12.3	66.1	7.2	5.5	2.5	100	13.1
45-49	2.4	11.3	66.5	9.1	6.2	4.4	100	19.8
50-54	1.2	11.0	62.1	11.1	8.1	6.6	100	17.7
55-59	0.7	12.8	55.6	11.0	9.9	10.1	100	5.5
60 and over	1.0	21.7	52.6	8.6	7.3	8.7	100	0.9
All ages	19.4	11.3	54.0	6.8	4.9	3.5	100	87.8
Special								
Under 25	100.0	-	-	-	-	-	100	-
25-29	79.4	9.5	10.6	-	0.5	-	100	0.2
30-34	38.2	10.5	46.1	0.3	3.9	1.0	100	0.3
35-39	11.3	3.0	70.3	1.9	7.7	5.8	100	0.5
40-44	4.1	2.2	69.0	3.0	11.3	10.3	100	0.9
45-49	1.6	1.3	62.7	3.6	13.1	17.7	100	1.4
50-54	1.2	0.8	61.4	2.9	12.3	21.5	100	1.1
55-59	0.3	1.3	52.9	3.6	12.0	29.9	100	0.3
60 and over	-	-	61.9	7.1	7.1	23.8	100	-
All ages	8.7	2.4	60.3	2.8	10.8	14.9	100	4.8
Total	20.0	10.9	46.8	5.1	7.3	9.9	100	122.1

Source: Database of Teacher Records.

1. Teachers not on a spine point are allocated to the nearest point according to their salary.
2. Provisional estimates.

TEACHERS PAY

32

Full-time regular qualified teachers in the maintained schools sector March 2000 by spine point[1] and age[2]

ENGLAND AND WALES ii. Women

	Percentage of teachers in each age band							Total numbers (thousands)
	Classroom teachers' pay spine[1]				Deputy heads	Heads	Total	
	0 - 8.5	9	9.5 - 13.5	14 - 17				
Nursery & Primary								
Under 25	99.9	-	-	-	-	-	100	9.5
25-29	91.1	5.1	3.1	-	0.6	-	100	25.8
30-34	34.0	23.9	33.7	0.1	7.1	1.3	100	17.2
35-39	27.5	22.4	34.2	0.1	10.8	5.0	100	13.0
40-44	19.6	25.8	35.9	0.1	10.0	8.7	100	19.1
45-49	6.3	29.0	42.4	0.2	10.4	11.7	100	31.2
50-54	2.2	27.9	45.0	0.2	9.8	15.0	100	25.9
55-59	1.0	25.5	45.2	0.3	9.3	18.6	100	8.9
60 and over	0.8	24.0	45.0	0.3	7.2	22.7	100	1.1
All ages	31.9	21.2	31.3	0.1	7.5	7.9	100	151.8
Secondary								
Under 25	99.9	-	-	-	-	-	100	4.6
25-29	87.7	6.1	6.2	-	-	-	100	17.4
30-34	37.3	16.6	44.7	1.1	0.3	-	100	12.4
35-39	16.5	16.1	61.2	3.7	2.2	0.3	100	10.5
40-44	8.8	16.2	65.3	4.9	3.6	1.2	100	15.2
45-49	4.0	18.0	67.3	5.0	3.6	2.0	100	20.3
50-54	1.6	18.4	68.4	5.2	4.0	2.4	100	15.6
55-59	0.7	19.6	67.2	5.3	4.1	3.1	100	5.6
60 and over	0.5	19.1	65.3	5.5	4.7	4.9	100	0.8
All ages	27.7	14.7	50.6	3.4	2.4	1.2	100	102.5
Special								
Under 25	100.0	-	-	-	-	-	100	0.1
25-29	77.8	10.1	12.1	-	-	-	100	0.6
30-34	24.0	8.6	63.0	0.1	3.6	0.7	100	0.8
35-39	11.0	4.3	72.8	1.1	7.5	3.4	100	0.9
40-44	6.1	2.0	75.3	1.8	8.9	5.9	100	1.8
45-49	2.7	1.7	80.7	1.7	7.2	6.0	100	2.6
50-54	1.7	0.5	79.0	2.4	7.8	8.6	100	2.2
55-59	0.6	0.2	79.8	2.4	6.6	10.3	100	0.8
60 and over	-	2.2	76.3	4.3	4.3	12.9	100	0.1
All ages	10.8	2.6	72.2	1.7	6.8	5.9	100	9.9
Total	29.5	18.0	40.3	1.4	5.5	5.3	100	264.1

Source: Database of Teacher Records.

1. Teachers not on a spine point are allocated to the nearest point according to their salary.
2. Provisional estimates.

TEACHERS PAY

32

Full-time regular qualified teachers in the maintained schools sector March 2000 by spine point[1] and age[2]

ENGLAND AND WALES · · · iii. All teachers

	Percentage of teachers in each age band							Total numbers (thousands)
	Classroom teachers' pay spine[1]				Deputy heads	Heads	Total	
	0 - 8.5	9	9.5 - 13.5	14 - 17				
Nursery & Primary								
Under 25	99.9	-	-	-	-	-	100	10.4
25-29	91.1	5.0	3.0	-	0.8	0.1	100	29.2
30-34	35.6	22.2	32.4	0.1	8.1	1.7	100	20.8
35-39	26.2	21.1	33.5	0.1	12.4	6.7	100	16.4
40-44	18.0	23.8	34.9	0.1	11.1	12.0	100	22.7
45-49	5.7	26.1	40.0	0.2	11.6	16.4	100	37.7
50-54	2.0	24.6	41.1	0.3	10.9	21.2	100	31.9
55-59	0.8	22.7	40.9	0.4	9.9	25.3	100	10.8
60 and over	0.7	21.8	41.3	0.3	7.8	28.0	100	1.4
All ages	30.5	19.6	30.0	0.2	8.6	11.2	100	181.4
Secondary								
Under 25	100.0	-	-	-	-	-	100	6.4
25-29	87.5	5.9	6.6	0.1	-	-	100	26.8
30-34	38.9	15.4	44.0	1.2	0.4	-	100	22.1
35-39	16.6	14.9	61.6	4.0	2.5	0.4	100	20.3
40-44	7.7	14.4	65.7	6.0	4.5	1.8	100	28.3
45-49	3.2	14.7	66.9	7.0	4.9	3.2	100	40.1
50-54	1.4	14.5	65.0	8.3	6.2	4.6	100	33.3
55-59	0.7	16.3	61.4	8.1	7.0	6.5	100	11.1
60 and over	0.8	20.5	58.6	7.1	6.0	6.9	100	1.7
All ages	23.9	13.2	52.2	5.0	3.6	2.2	100	190.2
Special								
Under 25	100.0	-	-	-	-	-	100	0.1
25-29	78.2	10.0	11.7	-	0.1	-	100	0.8
30-34	28.1	9.2	58.1	0.2	3.7	0.8	100	1.1
35-39	11.1	3.9	71.9	1.4	7.6	4.2	100	1.4
40-44	5.4	2.1	73.2	2.2	9.7	7.4	100	2.7
45-49	2.3	1.5	74.4	2.4	9.2	10.1	100	4.1
50-54	1.6	0.6	73.3	2.6	9.2	12.8	100	3.2
55-59	0.5	0.5	72.5	2.7	8.1	15.6	100	1.2
60 and over	-	1.5	71.9	5.2	5.2	16.3	100	0.1
All ages	10.1	2.6	68.4	2.0	8.1	8.8	100	14.7
Total	26.5	15.8	42.4	2.6	6.1	6.7	100	386.2

Source: Database of Teacher Records.

1. Teachers not on a spine point are allocated to the nearest point according to their salary.
2. Provisional estimates.

33

TEACHERS PAY

Full-time regular qualified classroom teachers in the maintained schools sector March 2000[1]: salary bands and average salary by phase, sex and age

ENGLAND AND WALES

	Under 17000	£17,000 -£22,999	£23,000 -£24999	£25,000 -£29,999	£30,000 and over	Salary unknown	Total	Average salary (£)
Nursery and primary								
Men								
Under 25	660	230	-	-	-	-	890	16,390
25-29	790	2,290	190	60	-	-	3,340	18,900
30-34	250	1,260	870	540	40	-	2,960	22,240
35-39	140	600	910	580	70	-	2,310	23,400
40-44	80	320	840	660	70	-	1,960	24,220
45-49	40	200	1,340	1,160	110	-	2,850	25,060
50-54	10	100	990	1,000	120	-	2,220	25,380
55 and over	-	10	290	330	40	-	670	25,700
All ages	1,960	5,010	5,430	4,340	460	10	17,200	22,650
Women								
Under 25	6,770	2,390	-	-	-	-	9,170	16,420
25-29	4,480	18,480	1,930	490	20	-	25,400	19,330
30-34	940	5,030	6,430	3,110	190	10	15,710	22,960
35-39	950	2,790	4,570	2,400	210	10	10,940	22,960
40-44	820	3,150	7,790	3,460	230	10	15,460	23,430
45-49	340	2,210	14,510	6,830	370	20	24,270	24,390
50-54	70	900	11,900	6,220	360	10	19,460	24,770
55 and over	10	210	4,160	2,670	170	10	7,210	25,060
All ages	14,380	35,160	51,280	25,180	1,540	70	127,610	22,470
Men and Women	16,340	40,180	56,700	29,520	2,010	70	144,810	22,490
Secondary								
Men								
Under 25	1,350	410	-	-	-	-	1,760	16,340
25-29	2,260	5,710	860	410	50	-	9,280	19,400
30-34	580	3,380	2,240	2,510	850	-	9,560	23,640
35-39	280	1,410	2,240	3,560	1,960	-	9,450	25,900
40-44	140	800	2,670	4,930	3,460	-	12,010	27,180
45-49	70	580	3,670	7,340	6,060	-	17,710	27,750
50-54	30	290	2,940	5,950	5,890	-	15,110	28,060
55 and over	10	70	1,230	1,850	1,990	-	5,150	27,940
All ages	4,720	12,650	15,850	26,540	20,250	10	80,020	25,790
Women								
Under 25	3,360	1,060	-	-	-	-	4,430	16,350
25-29	3,940	10,940	1,600	620	60	-	17,150	19,380
30-34	670	3,960	3,380	3,360	930	-	12,300	23,760
35-39	380	1,450	2,720	3,880	1,740	-	10,170	25,580
40-44	280	1,240	4,210	5,850	2,830	20	14,430	26,280
45-49	160	930	6,070	8,110	3,870	10	19,140	26,600
50-54	50	400	4,770	6,470	2,920	10	14,620	26,760
55 and over	10	110	1,990	2,630	1,210	-	5,950	26,830
All ages	8,850	20,080	24,740	30,920	13,560	40	98,180	24,390
Men and Women	13,570	32,730	40,590	57,460	33,810	50	178,200	25,020
Special and PRU	190	1,260	1,240	7,860	1,630	10	12,190	26,640
Maintained schools sector								
Men	6,730	18,000	21,600	33,020	21,400	20	100,760	25,310
Women	23,360	56,160	76,930	61,820	16,050	110	234,440	23,410
Men and Women	30,090	74,170	98,530	94,840	37,450	130	335,200	23,980

Source: Database of Teacher Records.

1. Provisional data.

34 TEACHERS PAY

Pay spine changes of full-time regular qualified teachers in maintained nursery and primary schools at March 2000[1,2]

ENGLAND AND WALES
(thousands)

	Position in March 1999								
	Head-teachers	Deputy head-teachers	Classroom teachers spine point				Other[3]	Not in service[4]	Total
			14 - 17	9.5 - 13.5	9	0 - 8.5			
Position in March 2000									
Headteachers	18.4	1.5	-	0.2	-	-	-	0.2	20.5
Deputy headteachers	0.3	13.2	-	1.6	0.2	0.2	-	0.2	15.8
Classroom teachers spine point									
14 - 17	-	-	0.1	-	-	-	-	-	0.2
9.5 - 13.5	0.1	0.6	-	46.3	5.1	1.3	-	1.1	54.4
9	-	0.1	-	1.8	25.7	4.7	-	3.0	35.3
0 - 8.5	-	-	-	-	0.1	41.7	0.1	13.1	55.1
All classroom teachers	0.1	0.7	0.1	48.2	30.9	47.7	0.2	17.2	145.1
Total	18.9	15.5	0.1	50.1	31.1	47.9	0.2	17.6	181.4

Percentage distribution of those in service in 2000 by their position in 1999

	1999				
2000	Head-teachers	Deputy head-teachers	Classroom & other	Not in service[4]	Total
Headteachers	90	8	1	1	100
Deputy headteachers	2	84	13	1	100
Classroom & other	-	-	88	12	100

Source: Database of Teacher Records.

1. Grossed up for those whose pay details are not yet available.
2. Provisional data.
3. Mainly teachers without qualified teacher status in 1999.
4. Not in full-time service in 1999.

TEACHERS PAY
Pay spine changes of full-time regular qualified teachers in maintained secondary schools at March 2000[1,2]

ENGLAND AND WALES   (thousands)

	Position in March 1999								
	Head-teachers	Deputy head-teachers	Classroom teachers spine point				Other[3]	Not in service[4]	Total
			14 - 17	9.5 - 13.5	9	0 - 8.5			
Position in March 2000									
Headteachers	3.8	0.3	-	-	-	-	-	0.1	4.2
Deputy headteachers	0.1	6.1	0.4	0.2	-	-	-	0.1	6.9
Classroom teachers spine point									
14 - 17	-	0.1	7.7	1.6	-	-	-	0.1	9.6
9.5 - 13.5	-	0.1	0.5	90.0	5.1	2.0	-	1.9	99.4
9	-	-	-	1.6	16.6	4.3	-	2.1	24.7
0 - 8.5	-	-	-	0.1	0.1	33.3	0.2	11.8	45.4
All classroom teachers	-	0.2	8.2	93.2	21.8	39.5	0.2	15.8	179.0
Total	3.9	6.6	8.6	93.5	21.8	39.5	0.3	16.0	190.2

Percentage distribution of those in service in 2000 by their position in 1999

2000	1999				
	Head-teachers	Deputy head-teachers	Classroom & other	Not in service[4]	Total
Headteachers	89	8	2	2	100
Deputy headteachers	2	88	9	1	100
Classroom & other	-	-	91	9	100

Source: Database of Teacher Records.

1. Grossed up for those whose pay details are not yet available.
2. Provisional data.
3. Mainly teachers without qualified teacher status in 1999.
4. Not in full-time service in 1999.

36

TEACHERS PAY
Full-time regular qualified teachers in maintained nursery, primary and secondary schools: School group by grade and classroom teacher spine point, March 2000[1]

ENGLAND[2]   (percentages)

| | School group[3] | | | | | | |
	1	2	3	4	5	6	Total
Heads	23	10	6	3	2	1	6
Deputy heads	9	9	6	4	3	3	6
Classroom teachers on spine point[4]							
0	-	-	-	-	-	-	-
0.5	-	-	-	-	-	-	-
1	-	-	-	-	-	-	-
1.5	-	-	-	-	-	-	-
2	5	5	4	4	4	3	4
2.5	-	-	-	-	-	-	-
3	4	5	5	4	4	3	4
3.5	-	-	-	-	-	-	-
4	4	5	4	4	4	4	4
4.5	-	-	-	-	-	-	-
5	4	4	4	3	3	3	4
5.5	-	-	-	-	-	-	-
6	3	4	4	3	3	3	3
6.5	-	-	-	-	-	-	-
7	3	4	4	3	3	3	3
7.5	-	-	-	-	-	-	-
8	3	3	3	3	3	3	3
8.5	-	-	-	-	-	-	-
9	20	20	18	12	13	14	16
9.5	2	1	1	1	1	1	1
10	13	14	15	10	9	10	12
10.5	1	1	1	1	1	-	1
11	4	10	15	15	14	13	12
11.5	-	-	1	1	1	1	1
12	-	1	5	13	12	11	7
12.5	-	-	-	1	1	1	-
13	-	-	1	11	14	13	7
13.5	-	-	-	1	1	-	-
14	-	-	-	3	5	5	2
14.5	-	-	-	-	-	-	-
15	-	-	-	-	-	-	-
15.5	-	-	-	-	-	-	-
16	-	-	-	-	-	-	-
16.5	-	-	-	-	-	-	-
17	-	-	-	-	-	-	-
Total	100	100	100	100	100	100	100

Source: Database of Teacher Records.

1. Provisional data.
2. School group information not available for Wales.
3. Group number of school that teachers are serving in. Data not available for groups 7 and 8.
4. Teachers not paid on a spine are allocated the nearest point according to their salary.

37

TEACHERS PAY
Full-time heads and deputy heads in maintained nursery, primary and secondary schools 1995 to 2000 by school group[1]

England and Wales (thousands)

	1995	1996	1997	1998[2]	1999[2]	2000[2]
Heads						
Nursery and primary						
School group						
1	7.0	6.9	6.8	6.6	6.3	6.6
2	10.8	10.8	10.6	10.6	10.3	9.5
3 - 8	3.2	3.3	3.4	3.5	3.7	4.1
Total	21.0	21.1	20.8	20.7	20.3	20.2
Secondary						
School group						
1	0.2	0.2	0.2	0.3	0.3	0.3
2	0.4	0.4	0.4	0.4	0.4	0.3
3	0.5	0.5	0.5	0.5	0.5	0.4
4	0.9	0.9	0.9	0.8	0.8	0.6
5	1.8	1.8	1.8	1.8	1.7	1.2
6	0.6	0.6	0.6	0.6	0.7	1.0
7	.	.	.	.	.	0.4
8	.	.	.	.	.	0.1
Total	4.4	4.4	4.3	4.3	4.3	4.2
Deputy heads						
Nursery and primary						
School group						
1	3.8	3.8	3.5	3.3	3.3	3.0
2	10.5	10.1	9.9	9.5	9.4	9.0
3 - 6	3.3	3.2	3.2	3.3	3.4	3.4
Total	17.7	17.2	16.6	16.1	16.1	15.4
Secondary						
School group						
1	0.1	0.1	0.1	0.1	0.1	0.2
2	0.4	0.4	0.3	0.3	0.3	0.3
3	0.5	0.5	0.5	0.5	0.5	0.4
4	1.5	1.5	1.4	1.3	1.3	1.2
5	4.1	3.8	3.5	3.3	3.2	3.1
6	1.4	1.4	1.4	1.4	1.4	1.5
Total	8.1	7.6	7.1	6.9	6.9	6.8

Source: Database of Teacher Records.

1. School group number on which salary is based.
2. Provisional 1999 and 2000 estimates. Excludes a small number whose school group information is not yet available.

TEACHERS PAY
Full-time regular qualified teachers March 2000[1]: spine point[2] distribution by phase, sex and length of service

38

ENGLAND AND WALES

	Percentage of teachers in each length of service band							
	Classroom teachers' pay spine[1]				Deputy heads	Heads	Total	Total numbers (thousands)
	0 - 8.5	9	9.5 - 13.5	14 - 17				
Nursery and primary								
Men								
0 - 4 years	94.1	3.2	1.8	-	0.1	0.8	100	6.4
5 - 9 years	21.6	27.0	36.1	0.1	12.2	3.0	100	4.3
10 - 14 years	0.5	15.7	41.5	0.4	24.4	17.5	100	2.9
15 - 19 years	0.3	13.3	32.2	0.4	19.9	34.0	100	1.9
20 + years	0.1	8.4	24.4	0.6	17.1	49.3	100	14.1
Total	23.3	11.1	23.5	0.4	13.8	28.0	100	29.6
Women								
0 - 4 years	96.0	2.5	1.2	-	0.2	0.1	100	42.9
5 - 9 years	27.8	33.4	32.4	0.1	5.2	1.1	100	26.5
10 - 14 years	0.9	34.5	47.4	0.1	11.2	5.8	100	19.3
15 - 19 years	0.3	30.7	47.5	0.2	11.4	10.0	100	21.4
20 + years	0.3	21.3	45.2	0.2	12.8	20.2	100	41.7
Total	31.9	21.2	31.3	0.1	7.5	7.9	100	151.8
Men and Women	30.5	19.6	30.0	0.2	8.6	11.2	100	181.4
Secondary								
Men								
0 - 4 years	88.4	6.1	5.3	0.1	-	-	100	17.4
5 - 9 years	15.1	25.7	57.6	1.1	0.4	0.1	100	12.0
10 - 14 years	0.3	18.0	73.1	5.0	3.0	0.6	100	8.2
15 - 19 years	0.2	12.1	72.4	7.3	5.6	2.3	100	10.3
20 + years	0.1	7.6	65.0	11.7	8.7	6.8	100	39.9
Total	19.4	11.3	54.0	6.8	4.9	3.5	100	87.8
Women								
0 - 4 years	92.8	4.1	3.1	-	-	-	100	27.7
5 - 9 years	18.7	27.1	52.9	0.9	0.4	0.1	100	15.8
10 - 14 years	0.6	22.7	71.5	3.1	1.6	0.4	100	12.6
15 - 19 years	0.2	18.3	72.5	4.7	3.2	1.1	100	16.7
20 + years	0.1	12.5	71.5	7.0	5.6	3.3	100	29.7
Total	27.7	14.7	50.6	3.4	2.4	1.2	100	102.5
Men and Women	23.9	13.2	52.2	5.0	3.6	2.2	100	190.2
Special and PRU								
Men								
0 - 4 years	68.6	9.2	21.5	-	0.7	-	100	0.6
5 - 9 years	5.0	8.5	81.1	1.0	4.0	0.4	100	0.5
10 - 14 years	0.4	0.6	81.0	2.8	9.4	5.8	100	0.5
15 - 19 years	0.3	0.8	71.8	2.6	11.3	13.2	100	0.8
20 + years	0.1	0.5	56.7	4.0	14.7	24.1	100	2.4
Total	8.7	2.4	60.3	2.8	10.8	14.9	100	4.8
Women								
0 - 4 years	78.3	7.3	14.0	0.1	0.2	0.2	100	1.2
5 - 9 years	8.1	10.2	78.0	0.4	2.9	0.4	100	1.4
10 - 14 years	0.4	1.2	88.6	1.0	6.2	2.5	100	1.6
15 - 19 years	0.1	0.6	83.2	2.1	8.5	5.5	100	2.2
20 + years	0.1	0.1	75.4	2.7	9.8	11.9	100	3.5
Total	10.8	2.6	72.2	1.7	6.8	5.9	100	9.9
Men and Women	10.1	2.6	68.4	2.0	8.1	8.8	100	14.7

Source: Database of Teacher Records.

1. Teachers not on a spine point are allocated to the nearest point according to their salary.
2. Provisional data

TEACHERS PAY
Average salary of full-time regular qualified teachers in the maintained schools sector by sex, grade, phase and age, March 2000[1]

ENGLAND AND WALES

	Men				Women			
	Head	Deputy head	Classroom	Total	Head	Deputy head	Classroom	Total
Nursery and primary								
Under 25	-	-	16,390	16,390	31,430	-	16,420	16,420
25-29	32,220	28,300	18,900	19,130	30,890	28,380	19,330	19,400
30-34	33,000	29,170	22,240	23,530	33,210	29,200	22,960	23,560
35-39	34,250	29,510	23,400	25,970	33,800	29,690	22,960	24,260
40-44	34,950	29,950	24,220	28,390	34,330	29,580	23,430	24,990
45-49	35,390	30,210	25,060	29,980	34,610	29,650	24,390	26,160
50-54	35,950	30,140	25,380	31,190	34,910	29,800	24,770	26,810
55-59	36,580	30,270	25,680	32,550	35,630	30,080	25,020	27,480
60 & over	37,880	31,400	25,790	32,660	37,010	30,570	25,340	28,390
all ages	35,620	29,910	22,650	27,300	34,800	29,650	22,470	24,010
Maintained secondary								
Under 25	-	-	16,340	16,340	-	15,540	16,350	16,350
25-29	-	27,290	19,400	19,410	-	27,830	19,380	19,380
30-34	33,520	35,710	23,640	23,710	36,370	34,960	23,760	23,800
35-39	43,410	36,790	25,900	26,300	40,170	36,490	25,580	25,870
40-44	46,810	37,010	27,180	28,230	44,000	36,650	26,280	26,870
45-49	47,380	37,430	27,750	29,210	45,550	37,070	26,600	27,350
50-54	49,650	37,740	28,060	30,260	47,840	37,280	26,760	27,700
55-59	50,960	38,310	28,060	31,410	46,810	37,740	26,810	27,890
60 & over	54,760	38,920	27,270	30,510	53,300	37,290	27,010	28,760
all ages	48,980	37,530	25,790	27,180	46,320	36,980	24,390	24,950
Special and PRU								
Under 25	-	-	17,280	17,280	-	-	17,260	17,260
25-29	-	29,050	20,870	20,920	-	-	21,120	21,120
30-34	36,770	31,810	24,100	24,560	37,590	30,830	24,960	25,240
35-39	39,500	33,130	26,880	28,100	36,700	31,860	26,320	27,090
40-44	40,770	33,090	27,860	29,830	38,310	32,530	26,900	28,060
45-49	41,210	33,310	28,370	31,250	39,110	31,990	27,080	28,130
50-54	41,100	33,710	28,120	31,560	38,320	32,810	27,340	28,700
55-59	43,830	33,460	29,210	33,960	40,120	32,710	27,560	29,210
60 & over	47,560	35,150	28,190	33,990	42,640	30,940	28,430	30,300
all ages	41,480	33,330	27,290	30,060	38,800	32,320	26,370	27,500
All sectors								
Under 25	-	-	16,360	16,360	31,430	15,540	16,400	16,400
25-29	32,220	28,260	19,300	19,360	30,890	28,360	19,370	19,420
30-34	33,100	29,930	23,330	23,680	33,360	29,420	23,360	23,700
35-39	35,390	31,850	25,460	26,280	34,190	30,690	24,310	25,060
40-44	37,910	33,680	26,820	28,350	35,430	31,240	24,900	25,930
45-49	38,640	34,000	27,420	29,490	35,780	31,040	25,450	26,700
50-54	39,920	34,690	27,740	30,540	36,140	31,350	25,710	27,220
55-59	41,550	35,780	27,840	31,800	36,830	31,810	25,920	27,720
60 & over	44,520	36,640	27,140	31,070	39,310	32,640	26,260	28,630
all ages	39,330	33,830	25,310	27,320	35,950	31,000	23,410	24,500

CONTINUED
TEACHERS PAY
Average salary of full-time regular qualified teachers in the maintained schools sector by sex, grade, phase and age, March 2000[1]

ENGLAND AND WALES

	Men and Women			
	Head	Deputy head	Classroom	Total
Nursery and primary				
Under 25	31,430	-	16,420	16,420
25-29	31,530	28,360	19,280	19,360
30-34	33,130	29,190	22,850	23,550
35-39	33,980	29,630	23,040	24,620
40-44	34,580	29,670	23,520	25,540
45-49	34,930	29,790	24,460	26,810
50-54	35,350	29,890	24,830	27,630
55-59	36,000	30,120	25,070	28,370
60 & over	37,300	30,790	25,390	29,180
all ages	35,130	29,720	22,490	24,540
Maintained secondary				
Under 25	-	15,540	16,350	16,350
25-29	-	27,630	19,390	19,390
30-34	35,800	35,380	23,710	23,760
35-39	42,190	36,650	25,730	26,080
40-44	45,820	36,850	26,690	27,500
45-49	46,810	37,300	27,150	28,270
50-54	49,200	37,600	27,420	29,060
55-59	49,980	38,140	27,380	29,630
60 & over	54,280	38,330	27,140	29,690
all ages	48,230	37,330	25,020	25,980
Special				
Under 25	-	-	17,260	17,260
25-29	-	29,050	21,060	21,070
30-34	37,240	31,150	24,710	25,050
35-39	38,020	32,290	26,500	27,430
40-44	39,530	32,750	27,210	28,670
45-49	40,430	32,640	27,470	29,240
50-54	39,850	33,190	27,560	29,630
55-59	42,070	33,010	27,920	30,550
60 & over	44,980	32,750	28,370	31,380
all ages	40,290	32,750	26,640	28,330
All sectors				
Under 25	31,430	15,540	16,400	16,400
25-29	31,530	28,330	19,360	19,400
30-34	33,260	29,560	23,350	23,690
35-39	34,700	31,090	24,720	25,500
40-44	36,520	32,120	25,510	26,730
45-49	37,100	32,150	26,080	27,650
50-54	37,980	32,780	26,390	28,420
55-59	39,070	33,470	26,480	29,080
60 & over	41,490	34,410	26,580	29,540
all ages	37,520	32,070	23,980	25,400

Source: Database of Teacher Records.

1. Data are provisional.

PROMOTIONS

40

Full-time regular qualified teachers promoted to head teacher in the maintained schools sector 1995-96 to 1999-2000 by grade[1], phase and sex

ENGLAND

	March 95 to March 96	March 96 to March 97	March 97 to March 98[2]	March 98 to March 99[2]	March 99 to March 00[2]
Promoted from classroom teachers:					
Nursery and primary					
Men	50	50	70	40	50
Women	230	270	340	250	190
All teachers	280	320	410	290	240
Secondary					
Men	40	60	70	60	30
Women	30	40	70	60	30
All teachers	70	90	150	120	60
Special and PRU					
Men	0	20	10	20	10
Women	10	20	30	30	10
All teachers	20	30	40	40	20
Promoted from deputy heads:					
Nursery and primary					
Men	460	450	500	280	430
Women	970	1,090	1,210	850	980
All teachers	1,430	1,540	1,700	1,130	1,410
Secondary					
Men	230	240	250	170	200
Women	90	120	140	110	120
All teachers	320	350	390	290	310
Special and PRU					
Men	50	50	50	40	40
Women	60	60	50	40	60
All teachers	110	110	110	80	100
Total promoted to head in the maintained schools sector					
Men	830	860	960	610	760
Women	1,400	1,590	1,840	1,330	1,390
All teachers	2,230	2,450	2,790	1,940	2,150

Source: Database of Teacher Records.

1. Those recorded as classroom or deputy head as at 31 March of one year and as head at 31 March the following year.
2. Provisional data.

TEACHER SICKNESS ABSENCE

Full-time and part-time teacher sickness absence in calendar year 2000 by local education authority[1]

ENGLAND

	Full-time (or full-time plus part-time if figures combined, see footnotes)			Part-time		
	Number taking absence	Total number of days taken	Days taken as part of absences of more than 20 days	Number taking absence	Total number of days taken	Days taken as part of absences of more than 20 days
Darlington	360	2,890	800	20	130	80
Hartlepool	520	6,330	3,430	30	100	30
Middlesbrough	730	7,610	3,760	60	730	380
Redcar and Cleveland	810	9,190	5,020	50	200	60
Stockton on Tees	1,070	16,350	10,410	90	1,420	910
Durham	1,460	16,350	9,250	150	1,000	440
Northumberland	1,320	15,330	5,230	180	1,820	570
Gateshead	1,720	11,630	6,060	110	930	570
Newcastle upon Tyne	1,400	16,350	10,610	120	1,350	940
North Tyneside	840	8,060	3,810	100	1,570	1,070
South Tyneside	880	12,280	7,440	30	510	370
Sunderland	1,640	19,100	10,220	80	1,130	670
North East	**12,760**	**141,460**	**76,030**	**1,010**	**10,890**	**6,080**
Blackburn with Darwen	380	5,280	3,740	50	1,020	870
Blackpool	770	8,370	1,590	100	1,330	530
Halton	790	7,280	2,630	50	520	320
Warrington	950	7,900	2,720	150	610	220
Cheshire	3,460	34,230	16,950	380	3,030	1,390
Cumbria	1,320	14,640	8,010	240	2,000	1,250
Bolton	1,600	15,130	1,570	180	3,240	620
Bury	890	8,770	4,070	80	570	270
Manchester	2,190	29,160	19,090	190	1,630	920
Oldham	1,350	16,200	7,450	120	1,180	580
Rochdale	1,270	17,120	9,980	100	1,250	740
Salford	1,310	16,040	8,890	80	840	430
Stockport	1,250	10,600	590	80	550	-
Tameside	1,220	14,260	7,380	100	1,770	1,250
Trafford	840	12,840	9,270	80	1,080	740
Wigan	1,670	18,450	9,820	140	1,170	530
Lancashire	5,580	50,000	22,230	740	7,210	2,810
Knowsley	1,040	11,890	6,650	70	570	170
Liverpool	1,600	14,530	5,420	110	780	300
St Helens[2]	..	..	..	..	..	..
Sefton	1,670	17,270	7,670	210	1,160	620
Wirral	1,690	20,550	9,430	260	2,930	1,990
North West[3]	**33,730**	**360,130**	**169,650**	**3,530**	**34,990**	**16,800**

41 **TEACHER SICKNESS ABSENCE**
Full-time and part-time teacher sickness absence in calendar year 2000 by local education authority[1]

ENGLAND

	Full-time (or full-time plus part-time if figures combined, see footnotes)			Part-time		
	Number taking absence	Total number of days taken	Days taken as part of absences of more than 20 days	Number taking absence	Total number of days taken	Days taken as part of absences of more than 20 days
East Riding of Yorkshire	1,540	17,610	7,200	190	2,060	1,010
City of Kingston Upon Hull	1,340	15,910	7,400	180	2,050	1,160
North East Lincolnshire	920	11,360	5,750	120	1,690	980
North Lincolnshire	830	9,630	5,030	100	1,180	660
York	760	7,470	3,520	50	290	100
North Yorkshire	3,110	30,920	14,360	610	5,120	2,450
Barnsley	960	11,840	9,690	110	440	250
Doncaster	1,690	19,360	10,050	200	2,890	1,810
Rotherham	840	7,130	2,070	280	2,570	750
Sheffield	2,540	30,340	15,560	540	5,690	3,290
Bradford[4]	2,970	41,700	24,580	..	..	..
Calderdale	970	10,160	4,640	90	560	160
Kirklees	2,400	27,870	10,880	310	3,380	1,510
Leeds	3,370	38,010	17,010	230	3,340	1,880
Wakefield	1,700	22,200	13,030	100	960	550
Yorkshire and the Humber[3]	**25,580**	**296,850**	**147,900**	**3,460**	**36,860**	**19,390**
Derby[4]	1,030	9,150	290	..	..	..
Leicester	1,880	18,610	8,440	260	1,690	510
Nottingham	1,270	13,520	6,260	130	1,000	270
Rutland	130	880	310	30	260	160
Derbyshire	3,070	37,290	19,450	580	4,280	1,700
Leicestershire	2,860	23,080	7,930	780	9,920	6,260
Lincolnshire[2]	..	..	..	..	..	..
Northamptonshire	3,210	28,460	11,020	440	3,940	1,510
Nottinghamshire	2,580	29,210	14,150	300	2,700	1,520
East Midlands[3]	**18,860**	**189,110**	**81,220**	**3,060**	**28,620**	**13,850**
Herefordshire	800	7,880	2,300	180	1,000	300
Stoke on Trent[4]	1,430	21,460	11,830	..	..	..
Telford and Wrekin	750	7,410	2,760	100	490	180
Shropshire	1,380	13,840	6,180	220	1,290	380
Staffordshire	3,960	48,340	26,110	380	3,580	1,510
Warwickshire	2,800	28,160	11,370	560	5,270	2,620
Birmingham[2]	..	..	..	..	..	..
Coventry	1,560	15,810	8,230	240	2,420	1,290
Dudley[2]	..	..	..	..	..	..
Sandwell[5]	1,840	20,600	8,820	170	..	..
Solihull[6]	1,550	10,230	..	..	..	..
Walsall	1,440	19,380	9,440	60	620	260
Wolverhampton	1,390	12,370	5,800	160	650	140
Worcestershire	2,790	30,500	16,860	420	4,990	3,080
West Midlands[3]	**29,440**	**318,230**	**154,650**	**3,550**	**32,750**	**15,610**

CONTINUED
TEACHER SICKNESS ABSENCE
Full-time and part-time teacher sickness absence in calendar year 2000 by local education authority[1]

41

ENGLAND

	Full-time (or full-time plus part-time if figures combined, see footnotes)			Part-time		
	Number taking absence	Total number of days taken	Days taken as part of absences of more than 20 days	Number taking absence	Total number of days taken	Days taken as part of absences of more than 20 days
Luton	910	7,620	1,950	130	1,200	460
Peterborough	650	7,670	3,500	110	3,210	2,650
Southend on Sea	880	6,740	2,530	70	570	260
Thurrock	920	9,590	3,870	70	430	160
Bedfordshire	1,790	16,780	7,440	220	1,300	260
Cambridgeshire	2,140	26,310	17,120	330	3,890	2,490
Essex	7,000	61,860	23,810	1,010	8,560	4,000
Hertfordshire	4,500	40,360	14,670	1,140	10,800	5,570
Norfolk	3,660	25,920	10,920	700	4,940	2,080
Suffolk	3,390	30,130	11,950	730	6,090	2,680
East of England	**25,830**	**232,970**	**97,750**	**4,490**	**40,980**	**20,610**
Camden	890	7,270	2,240	160	1,480	720
City of London	20	80	-	-	-	-
Hackney	1,150	11,880	1,310	230	2,950	370
Hammersmith and Fulham	630	5,490	2,240	100	510	80
Haringey	1,080	8,550	2,990	160	1,860	1,030
Islington[4]	1,070	7,550	1,690	..	..	..
Kensington and Chelsea	390	3,190	990	90	910	400
Lambeth	860	9,510	3,930	190	960	150
Lewisham	870	7,910	3,330	250	2,230	980
Newham	1,900	17,170	6,380	130	820	240
Southwark	1,080	10,970	4,310	100	970	570
Tower Hamlets	1,320	11,500	3,120	180	1,620	660
Wandsworth	1,060	8,210	2,930	180	1,140	350
City of Westminster	830	6,840	3,490	90	1,060	630
Barking and Dagenham	920	7,550	2,540	90	720	260
Barnet	1,460	12,690	4,450	330	3,050	1,630
Bexley	1,390	11,930	3,680	130	820	310
Brent	1,530	14,650	5,550	120	880	230
Bromley	1,650	7,430	1,710	100	700	220
Croydon	1,440	12,920	5,100	180	1,200	500
Ealing	1,700	15,130	5,560	170	940	170
Enfield[2]	..	..	..	..	..	..
Greenwich	1,290	12,410	5,500	220	1,340	290
Harrow	1,070	11,230	4,500	230	2,050	980
Havering[2]	..	..	..	..	..	..
Hillingdon	1,360	10,080	2,950	160	500	190
Hounslow	1,460	11,240	3,660	160	770	110
Kingston upon Thames	710	5,610	1,990	150	1,540	650
Merton	770	6,020	2,320	100	570	200
Redbridge	1,430	10,090	2,680	190	1,130	320
Richmond upon Thames	620	4,590	1,480	110	880	270
Sutton	1,230	7,550	3,230	160	1,130	470
Waltham Forest[2]	..	..	..	..	..	..
London[3]	**37,330**	**312,160**	**108,110**	**4,990**	**39,090**	**14,490**

CONTINUED
TEACHER SICKNESS ABSENCE
Full-time and part-time teacher sickness absence in calendar year 2000 by local education authority[1]

ENGLAND

	Full-time (or full-time plus part-time if figures combined, see footnotes)			Part-time		
	Number taking absence	Total number of days taken	Days taken as part of absences of more than 20 days	Number taking absence	Total number of days taken	Days taken as part of absences of more than 20 days
Bracknell Forest	460	2,660	670	100	450	130
Brighton and Hove	580	9,650	7,070	120	1,440	930
Isle of Wight	510	6,280	3,340	70	820	370
Medway	1,000	8,170	2,970	80	320	140
Milton Keynes	690	5,680	1,350	20	240	50
Portsmouth	850	10,100	5,470	120	910	480
Reading	450	4,670	2,000	50	550	320
Slough	590	5,800	1,650	100	1,240	610
Southampton	1,240	12,920	6,050	130	760	290
West Berkshire	650	5,110	610	190	730	70
Windsor and Maidenhead	670	5,270	2,110	130	710	320
Wokingham[4]	960	7,970	3,020	..	..	..
Buckinghamshire	2,300	21,300	6,090	420	3,140	830
East Sussex	1,900	15,910	4,410	320	1,930	850
Hampshire	5,980	54,550	24,640	770	4,970	1,980
Kent	6,050	50,840	20,550	690	4,500	1,610
Oxfordshire	1,370	2,680	230	1,430	2,420	240
Surrey	3,700	33,430	17,200	840	3,620	1,670
West Sussex[2]	..	..	..	..	..	..
South East[3]	**32,740**	**288,220**	**120,020**	**6,300**	**32,480**	**12,270**

TEACHER SICKNESS ABSENCE
Full-time and part-time teacher sickness absence in calendar year 2000 by local education authority[1]

41

ENGLAND

	Full-time (or full-time plus part-time if figures combined, see footnotes)			Part-time		
	Number taking absence	Total number of days taken	Days taken as part of absences of more than 20 days	Number taking absence	Total number of days taken	Days taken as part of absences of more than 20 days
Bath and North East Somerset	960	10,080	5,850	180	1,540	870
Bournemouth	760	7,740	4,300	130	1,030	450
City of Bristol[2]	..	..	..	..	..	..
North Somerset	980	9,310	4,420	170	2,000	1,320
Plymouth	1,210	16,620	7,910	170	2,710	1,540
Poole	520	6,120	2,150	80	830	240
South Gloucestershire	1,410	14,480	2,570	310	3,310	1,770
Swindon	1,110	8,460	3,510	110	700	270
Torbay	670	8,840	4,590	110	1,000	360
Cornwall[4]	2,440	36,750	21,700	..	..	..
Isles of Scilly	-	50	30	10	30	-
Devon	2,850	29,900	14,670	560	6,190	3,550
Dorset	1,810	16,930	4,160	330	3,340	1,130
Gloucestershire	1,620	22,540	14,080	370	4,380	2,770
Somerset[7]	3,030	..	..	570	..	..
Wiltshire[2]	..	..	..	..	..	..
South West[3]	**22,550**	**253,280**	**118,350**	**4,060**	**45,320**	**24,610**
England[3]	**238,820**	**2,392,400**	**1,073,670**	**34,450**	**301,970**	**143,710**

Source: DfES annual 618G survey

1. Sickness absence on working days, whether paid absence or not, of teachers with permanent contracts or contracts of over one month. The number of teachers taking sick leave includes an individual teacher only once however many periods of sickness absence they have had. The number of days taken as sick leave includes all periods of sick leave.
2. Complete teacher sickness absence data not available.
3. Regional and England totals have been grossed up for authorities that did not provide data or provided apparently inadequate data.
4. Separate full-time and part-time figures not available. The combined full-time and part-time figures are shown in the full-time columns.
5. For Sandwell separate full-time and part-time data are only available for the number of teachers taking sickness absence. Other figures are combined full-time and part-time.
6. For Solihull separate full-time-time and part-time figures, and breakdown into periods of days are not available.
7. For Somerset only the number of teachers taking sickness absence is available.

42

VACANCIES
Vacancy numbers and rates in maintained nursery, primary, secondary and special schools by LEA[1] and Government Office region: January 1996 to 2001

England and Wales

	Number of vacancies						Vacancy rate(%)		
	1996	1997	1998	1999	2000	2001	1999	2000	2001
Gateshead	0	10	7	9	5	6	0.6	0.3	0.4
Newcastle upon Tyne	4	6	9	19	10	19	0.9	0.5	0.9
North Tyneside	0	0	0	26	16	14	1.7	1.1	0.8
South Tyneside	2	0	2	1	1	0	0.1	0.1	0.0
Sunderland	13	17	15	11	13	20	0.4	0.5	0.8
Former Cleveland	36	..	..	..	..	..	..	..	..
Hartlepool	..	7	4	11	4	5	1.4	0.5	0.6
Middlesbrough	..	4	14	7	4	20	0.6	0.3	1.7
Redcar and Cleveland	..	8	12	7	5	18	0.6	0.4	1.5
Stockton on Tees	0	14	9	7	8	15	0.5	0.5	0.9
Former Durham	12	7	..	..	..	..	..	..	..
Darlington	..	..	20	2	3	8	0.1	0.4	1.1
Durham (post 1.4.97)	..	..	7	0	2	37	0.0	0.1	0.9
Northumberland	0	0	0	0	0	0	0.0	0.0	0.0
NORTH EAST	**67**	**73**	**99**	**100**	**71**	**162**	*0.5*	*0.3*	*0.8*
Cumbria	3	4	2	2	0	6	0.1	0.0	0.2
Former Cheshire	34	26	46	..	..	..	..	..	..
Cheshire (post 1.4.98)	..	..	..	15	25	25	0.3	0.5	0.5
Halton	..	..	..	4	6	6	0.3	0.6	0.6
Warrington	..	..	..	7	12	11	0.5	0.8	0.7
Bolton	1	1	2	2	1	7	0.1	0.1	0.3
Bury	0	4	1	1	1	4	0.1	0.1	0.3
Manchester	4	9	0	0	0	0	0.0	0.0	0.0
Oldham	11	22	15	9	14	16	0.4	0.7	0.7
Rochdale	2	12	13	6	4	5	0.3	0.2	0.3
Salford	1	7	0	1	3	4	0.1	0.2	0.2
Stockport	7	1	2	5	7	25	0.3	0.4	1.2
Tameside	7	5	7	5	2	23	0.3	0.1	1.3
Trafford	1	3	2	1	0	0	0.1	0.0	0.0
Wigan	11	15	8	17	13	11	0.7	0.5	0.4
Former Lancashire	32	33	42	..	..	..	..	..	..
Lancashire (post 1.4.98)	..	..	..	34	27	61	0.4	0.3	0.7
Blackburn with Darwen	..	..	..	14	15	19	1.1	1.2	1.6
Blackpool	..	..	..	4	9	5	0.4	0.9	0.5
Knowsley	5	4	14	7	16	12	0.5	1.0	0.8
Liverpool	1	1	4	12	2	0	0.3	0.1	0.0
St Helens	6	8	5	5	1	8	0.3	0.1	0.5
Sefton	4	4	1	2	9	15	0.1	0.4	0.6
Wirral	6	8	14	17	10	20	0.6	0.4	0.3
NORTH WEST	**136**	**167**	**178**	**170**	**177**	**283**	*0.3*	*0.3*	*0.5*

CONTINUED
VACANCIES
Vacancy numbers and rates in maintained nursery, primary, secondary and special schools by LEA[1] and Government Office region:
January 1996 to 2001
England and Wales

	Number of vacancies						Vacancy rate(%)		
	1996	1997	1998	1999	2000	2001	1999	2000	2001
Former Humberside	25	..	..	..	..	..	..	..	..
Kingston-Upon-Hull, City of	..	2	1	1	0	8	0.1	0.0	0.4
East Riding of Yorkshire	..	0	1	4	2	6	0.2	0.1	0.3
North East Lincolnshire	..	0	2	0	0	20	0.0	0.0	1.6
North Lincolnshire	..	6	2	7	10	10	0.6	0.9	0.8
Former North Yorkshire	13	..	..	..	..	..	..	..	..
North Yorkshire (post 1.4.96)	..	..	18	8	10	12	0.2	0.2	0.3
York	..	..	..	8	6	6	0.7	0.5	0.5
Barnsley	..	1	7	2	2	20	0.1	0.1	1.3
Doncaster	..	1	0	0	2	10	0.0	0.1	0.4
Rotherham	..	0	0	1	1	1	0.0	0.0	0.0
Sheffield	14	13	21	2	8	14	0.1	0.2	0.4
Bradford	1	2	52	20	42	0	0.5	1.0	0.0
Calderdale	5	20	14	5	3	7	0.3	0.2	0.4
Kirklees	4	2	6	3	3	10	0.1	0.1	0.3
Leeds	16	10	28	10	21	47	0.2	0.4	0.8
Wakefield	..	..	..	..	2	14	..	0.1	0.5
YORKSHIRE AND THE HUMBER	**78**	**57**	**152**	**71**	**112**	**185**	**0.2**	**0.3**	**0.5**
Former Derbyshire	40	33	..	..	..	..	..	..	..
Derbyshire (post 1.4.97)	..	..	41	24	39	45	0.5	0.8	0.9
Derby	..	..	11	19	20	16	1.2	1.2	0.9
Former Leicestershire	22	34	..	..	..	..	0.0	..	..
Leicestershire	..	..	11	13	16	30	0.3	0.4	0.7
Leicester	..	..	13	14	21	42	0.6	0.9	1.8
Rutland	..	..	2	1	2	0	0.5	0.9	0.0
Lincolnshire	24	34	61	25	22	20	0.5	0.5	0.4
Northamptonshire	1	1	3	6	11	20	0.1	0.2	0.4
Former Nottinghamshire	0	0	0	..	..	..	..	..	..
Nottinghamshire (post 1.4.98)	..	..	..	0	0	0	0.0	0.0	0.0
Nottingham	..	..	..	0	25	41	0.0	1.3	2.2
EAST MIDLANDS	**87**	**102**	**142**	**102**	**156**	**214**	**0.3**	**0.5**	**0.7**

CONTINUED
VACANCIES

Vacancy numbers and rates in maintained nursery, primary, secondary and special schools by LEA[1] and Government Office region: January 1996 to 2001

England and Wales

	Number of vacancies						Vacancy rate(%)		
	1996	1997	1998	1999	2000	2001	1999	2000	2001
Former Hereford and Worcester	4	5	7	..	..	..	..	..	..
Herefordshire	..	..	..	6	12	18	0.5	1.1	1.6
Worcestershire	..	..	..	12	6	8	0.3	0.2	0.2
Former Shropshire	3	3	1	..	..	..	..	..	..
Shropshire (post 1.4.98)	..	..	..	1	2	4	0.1	0.1	0.2
Telford & Wrekin	..	..	..	0	17	5	0.0	1.4	0.4
Former Staffordshire	19	26	..	..	..	..	..	..	..
Staffordshire (post 1.4.97)	..	..	21	25	34	40	0.4	0.5	0.6
Stoke-on-Trent	..	..	18	3	23	20	0.2	1.3	1.1
Warwickshire	4	10	13	16	14	42	0.4	0.4	1.2
Birmingham	24	32	37	73	63	83	0.8	0.7	0.9
Coventry	23	14	7	13	23	24	0.5	0.9	1.0
Dudley	8	9	17	9	18	28	0.4	0.7	1.1
Sandwell	12	23	15	29	15	49	1.1	0.6	2.0
Solihull	12	5	8	3	14	32	0.2	0.8	1.7
Walsall	19	9	37	13	8	17	0.5	0.4	0.7
Wolverhampton	6	14	9	36	15	32	1.8	0.7	1.6
WEST MIDLANDS	**134**	**150**	**190**	**239**	**264**	**402**	**0.6**	**0.7**	**0.9**
Former Cambridgeshire	13	6	8	..	..	..	0.0	..	..
Cambridgeshire (post 1.4.98)	..	..	..	1	0	3	0.0	0.0	0.1
Peterborough	..	..	..	2	0	7	0.1	0.0	0.5
Norfolk	28	31	31	56	31	71	1.0	0.6	1.3
Suffolk	29	36	25	38	23	89	0.8	0.5	1.8
Former Bedfordshire	20	39	0	0	..	..	0.0	..	..
Bedfordshire (post 1.4.97)	0	0	26	26	45	76	0.8	1.5	2.6
Luton	0	0	25	24	14	63	1.7	0.9	4.2
Former Essex	70	86	106	..	..	..	0.0	..	..
Essex (post 1.4.98)	..	..	..	89	166	220	0.9	1.8	2.3
Southend-on-Sea	..	..	..	11	21	24	1.0	1.8	2.0
Thurrock	..	..	..	21	28	69	2.1	2.8	6.9
Hertfordshire	40	35	73	38	17	50	0.5	0.2	0.6
EAST OF ENGLAND	**200**	**233**	**294**	**306**	**345**	**672**	**0.8**	**0.7**	**1.7**

CONTINUED
VACANCIES
Vacancy numbers and rates in maintained nursery, primary, secondary and special schools by LEA[1] and Government Office region:
January 1996 to 2001
England and Wales

	Number of vacancies						Vacancy rate(%)		
	1996	1997	1998	1999	2000	2001	1999	2000	2001
City of London	0	1	0	1	1	0	7.7	7.7	0.0
Camden	13	23	19	37	31	59	3.1	2.7	5.2
Greenwich	26	24	58	62	35	63	3.6	2.0	3.6
Hackney	26	28	63	74	74	101	5.5	5.4	8.0
Hammersmith and Fulham	11	29	53	24	25	49	3.0	3.0	5.9
Islington	18	18	44	13	31	56	1.1	2.6	5.0
Kensington and Chelsea	0	0	20	9	5	36	1.7	0.9	6.6
Lambeth	25	29	12	60	56	51	4.3	4.1	3.7
Lewisham	33	31	52	31	42	71	2.0	2.6	4.2
Southwark	12	26	60	65	73	100	4.0	4.4	6.0
Tower Hamlets	19	64	66	97	100	157	5.0	5.4	8.6
Wandsworth	26	36	49	41	31	53	2.8	2.1	3.7
Westminster	23	19	21	29	34	49	2.9	3.3	4.8
Barking and Dagenham	8	43	19	19	17	24	1.4	1.2	1.7
Barnet	21	18	22	36	53	100	1.5	2.3	4.4
Bexley	4	5	8	7	33	85	0.4	1.9	4.8
Brent	13	27	35	31	12	23	1.6	0.6	1.2
Bromley	13	13	15	14	14	63	0.7	0.7	2.9
Croydon	15	25	20	37	40	77	1.7	1.6	3.2
Ealing	23	24	52	59	37	66	2.9	1.8	3.4
Enfield	10	10	20	30	30	65	1.3	1.3	2.7
Haringey	27	42	30	36	36	43	2.1	2.1	2.5
Harrow	9	5	12	19	46	58	1.4	3.9	4.5
Havering	10	9	15	13	18	38	0.8	1.1	2.2
Hillingdon	20	21	29	28	24	52	1.5	1.2	2.7
Hounslow	15	14	23	18	10	18	1.0	0.6	1.0
Kingston upon Thames	9	4	6	9	8	23	1.0	0.9	2.5
Merton	0	10	8	12	18	18	1.1	1.8	1.7
Newham	78	100	83	37	57	103	1.7	2.6	4.6
Redbridge	8	4	23	20	9	40	1.0	0.5	2.0
Richmond upon Thames	7	3	4	5	15	30	0.6	1.8	3.5
Sutton	6	5	10	9	1	10	0.7	0.1	0.7
Waltham Forest	6	41	48	7	4	7	0.4	0.2	0.4
LONDON	**534**	**751**	**999**	**989**	**1,020**	**1,788**	**2.0**	**2.0**	**3.5**

VACANCIES
Vacancy numbers and rates in maintained nursery, primary, secondary and special schools by LEA[1] and Government Office region:
January 1996 to 2001
England and Wales

	Number of vacancies						Vacancy rate(%)		
	1996	1997	1998	1999	2000	2001	1999	2000	2001
Former Berkshire	11	6	5	..	..	..	..	..	..
Bracknell Forest	..	..	..	0	10	16	0.0	1.5	2.4
Windsor and Maidenhead	..	..	..	9	15	34	1.0	1.7	3.9
West Berkshire	..	..	..	2	5	10	0.2	0.4	0.9
Reading	..	..	..	2	19	37	0.2	2.3	4.4
Slough	..	..	..	19	14	62	2.1	1.5	6.7
Wokingham	..	..	..	17	15	18	1.6	1.4	1.6
Former Buckinghamshire	33	40	..	..	..	..	..	..	..
Buckinghamshire (post 1.4.97)	..	..	35	40	55	59	1.2	1.6	1.8
Milton Keynes	..	..	9	13	7	21	0.8	0.4	1.3
Former East Sussex	30	31	..	..	..	..	..	..	..
East Sussex (post 1.4.97)	..	..	32	23	27	43	0.8	0.9	1.4
Brighton and Hove	..	..	13	4	11	17	0.3	0.8	1.1
Former Hampshire	66	81	..	..	..	..	..	..	..
Hampshire (post 1.4.97)	..	..	65	96	149	175	1.2	1.9	2.2
Portsmouth	..	..	23	16	19	59	1.2	1.5	4.5
Southampton	..	..	20	15	26	50	1.0	1.7	3.4
Isle of Wight	0	0	0	1	1	7	0.1	0.1	0.7
Former Kent	110	108	107	..	..	..	..	..	..
Kent (post 1.4.98)	..	..	..	98	93	196	1.0	0.9	2.0
Medway	..	..	..	17	16	51	0.8	0.8	2.6
Oxfordshire	..	1	7	11	8	16	0.3	0.2	0.4
Surrey	18	47	47	23	39	104	0.4	0.6	1.6
West Sussex	24	42	41	21	40	82	0.4	0.8	1.6
SOUTH EAST	**292**	**356**	**404**	**427**	**569**	**1,057**	**0.8**	**1.0**	**2.0**
Isles of Scilly	0	1	0	0	0	0	0.0	0.0	0.0
Former Avon	32	0	0	0	..	..	0.0	..	..
Bath and North East Somerset	..	4	5	5	4	9	0.4	0.3	0.7
City of Bristol	..	15	16	19	19	25	0.8	0.8	1.0
North Somerset	..	9	12	10	14	7	0.8	1.1	0.5
South Gloucestershire	..	13	9	5	3	7	0.3	0.2	0.4
Cornwall	2	9	8	9	11	0	0.3	0.3	0.0
Former Devon	16	26	24	0	..	..	0.0	..	..
Devon (post 1.4.98)	..	..	..	8	29	47	0.2	0.7	1.1
Plymouth	..	..	..	5	23	1	0.3	1.2	0.0
Torbay	..	..	..	3	7	9	0.4	0.9	1.0
Former Dorset	0	..	0	..	..	..	0.0	..	..
Dorset (post 1.4.97)	..	0	16	2	21	18	0.1	0.8	0.7
Poole	..	0	5	5	2	19	0.5	0.2	2.0
Bournemouth	..	0	0	2	2	7	0.2	0.2	0.7
Gloucestershire	13	14	9	9	26	14	0.2	0.7	0.3
Somerset	5	0	4	11	10	11	0.4	0.3	0.3
Former Wiltshire	13	21	..	..	..	..	0.0	..	..
Wiltshire (post 1.4.97)	..	..	19	21	14	19	0.8	0.5	0.7
Swindon	..	..	7	11	11	20	0.8	0.8	1.5
SOUTH WEST	**81**	**112**	**134**	**125**	**196**	**213**	**0.4**	**0.6**	**0.6**
ENGLAND	**1,609**	**2,001**	**2,592**	**2,529**	**2,910**	**4,976**	**0.7**	**0.8**	**1.4**

CONTINUED
VACANCIES
Vacancy numbers and rates in maintained nursery, primary, secondary and special schools by LEA[1] and Government Office region:
January 1996 to 2001
England and Wales

	Number of vacancies						Vacancy rate(%)		
	1996	1997	1998	1999	2000	2001	1999	2000	2001
Clwyd	3	..	..	..	..	..	..	..	..
Dyfed	13	..	..	..	..	..	..	..	..
Gwent	0	..	..	..	..	..	..	..	..
Gwynedd	6	..	..	..	..	..	..	..	..
Mid Glamorgan	47	..	..	..	..	..	..	..	..
Powys	5	..	..	..	..	..	..	..	..
South Glamorgan	0	..	..	..	..	..	..	..	..
West Glamorgan	14	..	..	..	..	..	..	..	..
Anglesey	..	2	2	3	4	3	0.5	0.7	0.5
Gwynedd	..	3	6	5	2	3	0.5	0.2	0.3
Conwy	..	1	3	2	0	4	0.3	0.0	0.5
Denbighshire	..	0	2	1	0	0	0.1	0.0	0.0
Flintshire	..	10	5	3	2	4	0.3	0.2	0.3
Wrexham	..	8	2	9	7	8	1.0	0.8	0.9
Powys	..	6	10	9	0	0	0.9	0.0	0.0
Ceredigion	..	0	0	0	0	0	0.0	0.0	0.0
Pembrokeshire	..	0	11	3	3	2	0.3	0.3	0.2
Carmarthenshire	..	15	23	14	1	2	1.0	0.1	0.1
Swansea	..	5	4	10	3	8	0.5	0.2	0.4
Neath & Port Talbot	..	9	4	7	2	6	0.6	0.2	0.5
Bridgend	..	12	12	15	10	6	1.2	0.8	0.5
Vale of Glamorgan	..	0	14	14	8	11	1.3	0.9	1.2
Rhondda Cynon Taff	..	10	41	20	15	32	0.9	0.7	1.4
Methyr Tydfil	..	0	1	0	0	0	0.0	0.0	0.0
Caerphilly	..	11	15	11	10	8	0.7	0.7	0.5
Blaenau Gwent	..	3	5	4	0	0	0.7	0.0	0.0
Torfaen	..	0	1	1	0	2	0.1	0.0	0.3
Monmouthshire	..	0	0	1	0	0	0.2	0.0	0.0
Newport	..	0	0	0	0	1	0.0	0.0	0.1
Cardiff	..	0	9	0	0	0	0.0	0.0	0.0
WALES	**88**	**95**	**170**	**132**	**67**	**100**	**0.5**	**0.3**	**0.4**
ENGLAND AND WALES	**1,697**	**2,110**	**2,762**	**2,661**	**2,977**	**5,076**	**0.7**	**0.8**	**1.3**

Source: DfES annual 618G survey and National Assembly for Wales annual stats3 survey.

1. The first, second and third phases of local government reorganisation came into effect on 1 April 1996, 1 April 1997 and 1 April 1998 respectively. The new authorities are shown directly below their former parent local education authorities.

43

VACANCIES
Vacancy rates[1] in maintained nursery and primary schools January 1996 to 2001[2], by grade and Government Office region

ENGLAND AND WALES

	Vacancies as a percentage of teachers in post[3]						Number of vacancies		
	1996	1997	1998	1999	2000	2001	1999	2000	2001
By grade (England only):									
Head or deputy head	0.8	0.9	1.4	1.3	1.0	1.2	447	367	424
Head	0.6	0.6	1.0	0.9	0.8	0.8	185	157	150
Deputy head	1.1	1.3	2.0	1.7	1.3	1.8	262	210	274
Classroom teachers	0.4	0.5	0.6	0.7	0.8	1.2	929	1,053	1,686
By Government office region:									
North East	0.3	0.4	0.4	0.5	0.3	0.6	48	29	57
North West	0.3	0.3	0.3	0.3	0.3	0.4	92	75	111
Yorkshire and The Humber	0.2	0.1	0.4	0.2	0.3	0.3	42	49	64
East Midlands	0.4	0.4	0.5	0.4	0.6	0.7	51	83	95
West Midlands	0.2	0.2	0.4	0.7	0.6	0.7	135	124	141
East of England	0.6	0.7	0.7	0.8	0.9	1.7	147	165	313
London	1.2	1.7	2.5	2.3	2.0	3.3	589	520	821
South East	0.6	0.8	0.8	0.8	1.0	1.6	201	269	420
South West	0.3	0.5	0.6	0.4	0.7	0.6	69	106	88
England	0.5	0.6	0.8	0.8	0.8	1.2	1,374	1,420	2,110
Wales	0.3	0.5	0.8	0.4	0.2	0.3	48	25	38
England and Wales	0.5	0.6	0.8	0.8	0.8	1.1	1,422	1,445	2,148
Inner London Weighting Area	1.6	2.4	3.5	3.4	2.9	4.2	481	401	568
Outer London Weighting Area	0.7	0.9	1.1	0.9	1.0	2.2	108	119	253

Source: DfES annual 618G survey and National Assembly for Wales stats3 survey.

1. Advertised vacancies for full-time permanent appointments (or appointments of at least one term's duration). Includes vacancies being filled on a temporary basis.
2. Excluding sixth form colleges.
3. Teachers in post include full-time regular teachers in (or on secondment from) maintained nursery and primary schools plus the nursery and primary portion of full-time regular divided service, peripatetic, advisory, and miscellaneous teachers.

VACANCIES

44

Vacancy[1] rates in maintained secondary schools, January 1995 to 2000[2], by grade and Government Office region

ENGLAND AND WALES

	Vacancies as a percentage of teachers in post[3]						Number of vacancies		
	1996	1997	1998	1999	2000	2001	1999	2000	2001
By grade (England only):									
Head or deputy head	0.7	0.7	1.0	1.0	1.0	1.0	104	103	109
Head	0.6	0.8	0.9	1.0	1.1	0.8	42	44	32
Deputy head	0.7	0.7	1.1	1.0	0.9	1.2	62	59	77
Classroom teachers	0.3	0.4	0.5	0.5	0.7	1.5	835	1,143	2,477
By Government office region:									
North East	0.3	0.3	0.4	0.5	0.4	1.0	46	37	104
North West	0.2	0.3	0.2	0.2	0.3	0.6	59	80	153
Yorkshire and The Humber	0.1	0.2	0.4	0.1	0.3	0.6	23	57	114
East Midlands	0.2	0.2	0.4	0.3	0.4	0.6	45	60	100
West Midlands	0.4	0.4	0.5	0.4	0.5	1.1	86	111	236
East of England	0.4	0.4	0.7	0.7	0.8	1.7	133	159	338
London	0.7	1.0	1.3	1.4	1.8	3.8	318	413	881
South East	0.5	0.5	0.6	0.7	1.0	2.1	187	250	548
South West	0.1	0.3	0.3	0.3	0.5	0.7	42	79	112
England	0.3	0.4	0.6	0.5	0.7	1.4	939	1,246	2,586
Wales	0.4	0.3	0.5	0.7	0.3	0.5	80	41	59
England and Wales	0.3	0.4	0.6	0.5	0.7	1.4	1,019	1,287	2,645
Inner London Weighting Area	0.9	1.6	1.7	1.8	2.3	4.4	197	256	495
Outer London Weighting Area	0.5	0.5	0.8	1.0	1.3	3.2	121	157	386

Source: DfES annual 618G survey and National Assembly for Wales stats3 survey.

1. Advertised vacancies for full-time permanent appointments (or appointments of at least one term's duration). Includes vacancies being filled on a temporary basis.
2. Excluding sixth form colleges.
3. Teachers in post include full-time regular teachers in (or on secondment from) maintained secondary schools plus the secondary portion of full-time regular divided service, peripatetic, advisory, and miscellaneous teachers.

ENGLAND

	Vacancies as a percentage of teachers in post[1,2]							Number of vacancies		
	1996	1997 (old)	1997 (new)	1998	1999	2000	2001	1999	2000	2001
Mathematics	0.2	0.4	0.4	0.7	0.8	1.2	2.1	143	233	410
Information technology	0.5	0.7	0.4	0.7	0.9	1.3	2.8	40	56	124
All Sciences[3]:	0.3	0.3	0.3	0.4	0.5	0.6	1.6	123	156	398
Chemistry	0.4	0.5	..	..	..	..	..	..	..	..
Physics	0.5	0.4	..	..	..	..	..	..	..	..
Biology	0.1	0.2	..	..	..	..	..	..	..	..
Other and combined science	0.2	0.3	..	..	..	..	..	..	..	..
Languages	0.5	0.6	0.5	0.7	0.5	0.7	1.5	79	109	245
English	0.4	0.3	0.4	0.4	0.5	0.7	1.8	83	129	360
Drama	0.4	0.7	0.5	0.2	0.4	0.7	1.7	14	23	59
History	0.2	0.1	0.1	0.2	0.2	0.2	0.5	15	12	39
Social sciences	-	0.4	0.2	-	0.1	0.2	0.4	4	8	15
Geography	0.2	0.3	0.3	0.4	0.1	0.3	0.6	8	25	51
Religious education	0.6	0.5	0.4	0.8	0.5	0.7	1.8	24	36	96
Design and technology	0.2	0.3	0.4	0.7	0.6	0.7	1.3	99	110	206
Commercial / business studies	-	0.4	0.4	0.6	0.4	0.5	1.3	12	17	41
Art, craft or design	0.3	0.2	0.2	0.3	0.5	0.3	0.7	34	24	47
Music	0.3	0.8	0.8	0.7	0.7	0.8	1.8	30	35	78
Physical education	0.2	0.2	0.2	0.3	0.3	0.2	0.8	29	30	102
Special Educational Needs[4]	1.1	1.2	1.1	..	..	..	..	..	..	..
Careers	0.5	1.0	1.0	1.8	0.9	1.4	4.3	2	3	9
Other main and combined subjects[4]	0.8	0.9	0.7	0.7	0.8	1.2	1.7	96	137	197
Total classroom teachers	0.3	0.4	0.4	0.5	0.5	0.7	1.5	835	1,143	2,477

Source: DfES annual 618G survey and National Assembly for Wales stats3 survey.

1. Teachers in post include full-time regular teachers in (or on secondment from) maintained secondary schools, plus the secondary portion of full-time regular divided service, peripatetic, advisory and miscellaneous teachers.
2. The number of teachers in post by main teaching subject is estimated using the 1992 Secondary School Staffing Survey for years 1996 - 1997 (old) and the 1996 Secondary Schools Curriculum and Staffing Survey for 1997 (new) to 2001.
3. Vacancies advertised in single sciences may be for combined science classes. The distinction between single science vacancies and combined science has been discontinued from 1997 (new).
4. Special Educational Needs has been included in 'other main and combined subjects' from 1997 (new).

RETIREMENTS

46

Retirements from the maintained schools sector[1]: Type of award and sex by year of award

ENGLAND

Financial year (1 April to 31 March)	Premature[2]			Age			Ill-health[3]			Total		
	Men	Women	Men and Women	Men	Women	Men and Women	Men	Women	Men and Women	Men	Women	Men and Women
1989-90	3,220	4,840	8,060	960	2,550	3,500	1,270	2,310	3,580	5,440	9,700	15,140
1990-91	3,000	4,740	7,740	890	2,610	3,500	1,420	2,860	4,280	5,310	10,210	15,520
1991-92	2,470	4,070	6,530	810	2,360	3,170	1,390	2,640	4,030	4,660	9,070	13,730
1992-93	2,760	4,400	7,170	750	2,560	3,310	1,440	2,610	4,050	4,950	9,580	14,530
1993-94	3,180	4,860	8,030	850	2,580	3,430	1,840	2,990	4,820	5,860	10,420	16,290
1994-95	2,730	4,390	7,120	780	2,740	3,520	1,970	3,310	5,290	5,490	10,440	15,930
1995-96	3,360	5,240	8,600	760	2,720	3,480	1,870	3,290	5,160	5,990	11,250	17,240
1996-97	3,840	6,370	10,210	690	2,590	3,270	1,810	3,170	4,980	6,340	12,120	18,460
1997-98[2]	4,400	7,090	11,490	740	2,730	3,480	1,210	2,090	3,300	6,360	11,910	18,270
1998-99	970	1,450	2,420	750	2,810	3,560	860	1,460	2,320	2,580	5,720	8,300
1999-00	1,150	1,530	2,670	870	3,090	3,960	870	1,480	2,350	2,880	6,100	8,980
2000-01[2,4]	1,280	1,920	3,190	890	2,990	3,880	1,040	1,580	2,610	3,200	6,480	9,680

Source: Pensioner Statistical System (PENSTATS).

1. Excludes sixth form colleges.
2. The effect of the change in the Teachers' Pension Scheme as from 31 August 1997 was that many more teachers took early retirement in 1997 than in previous years. Premature includes Actuarially Reduced Benefit retirements from 2000-01.
3. Changes in the statutory regulations governing ill-health retirement came into force on 1 April 1997. To qualify for ill-health retirement benefits a teacher must now be regarded as permanently unfit to teach.
4. 2000-01 data are provisional.

RETIREMENTS

Retirements: Type of award by last known sector[1] of service and sex: 2000-01[2]

47

ENGLAND

	Premature	Actuarially Reduced Benefit	Age	Ill-health	Total
Nursery and primary					
Men	320	40	190	330	890
Women	890	250	1,500	910	3,560
Total	1,210	300	1,690	1,250	4,450
Secondary					
Men	760	90	670	630	2,150
Women	540	140	1,370	570	2,620
Total	1,310	230	2,040	1,200	4,770
Special and PRU					
Men	50	-	30	70	160
Women	70	20	120	100	300
Total	120	30	150	170	470
Maintained schools sector					
Men	1,140	140	890	1,040	3,200
Women	1,500	420	2,990	1,580	6,480
Total	2,640	550	3,880	2,610	9,680
Other sectors[3]					
Men	200	130	1,110	310	1,750
Women	120	140	960	310	1,530
Total	320	270	2,070	620	3,280
Total					
Men	1,340	260	2,000	1,350	4,960
Women	1,620	560	3,950	1,890	8,010
Total	2,960	820	5,950	3,240	12,960

Source: Pensioner Statistical System (PENSTATS).

1. The last known sector of a teacher may have been some years prior to retirement date.
2. Provisional data.
3. Including those from independent schools and further and higher education establishments covered by the Teachers Pension Scheme.

RETIREMENTS
Retirements: Type of award by last known sector[1] of service and grade: 1999-00[2]

ENGLAND

	Premature	Actuarially Reduced Benefit	Age	Ill-health	Total
Nursery and primary					
Head teachers	430	50	290	250	1,030
Deputy heads	120	30	130	100	370
Classroom teachers	660	220	1,270	890	3,040
Others	10	-	10	-	20
Total	1,210	300	1,690	1,250	4,450
Secondary					
Head teachers	150	10	70	40	270
Deputy heads	120	10	70	40	240
Classroom teachers	1,030	210	1,860	1,100	4,200
Others	10	-	40	10	60
Total	1,310	230	2,040	1,200	4,770
Special and PRU					
Head teachers	20	-	20	20	60
Deputy heads	20	-	-	20	40
Classroom teachers	80	30	120	130	360
Others	-	-	-	-	10
Total	120	30	150	170	470
Maintained schools sector					
Head teachers	600	60	380	320	1,350
Deputy heads	260	40	190	160	650
Classroom teachers	1,760	450	3,260	2,130	7,600
Others	20	-	50	10	80
Total	2,640	550	3,880	2,610	9,680
Other sectors[3]					
Head teachers	-	-	10	-	10
Deputy heads	-	-	-	-	10
Classroom teachers	320	260	2,060	620	3,250
Others	-	-	-	-	-
Total	320	270	2,070	620	3,280
Total					
Head teachers	600	60	390	320	1,370
Deputy heads	260	40	200	160	660
Classroom teachers	2,080	720	5,310	2,750	10,850
Others	20	-	50	10	80
Total	2,960	820	5,950	3,240	12,960

Source: Database of Teacher Records and Pensioner Statistical System (PENSTATS).

1. The last known sector of a teacher may have been some years prior to retirement date.
2. Provisional data.
3. Including those from independent schools and further and higher education establishments covered by the Teachers Pension Scheme.

RETIREMENTS

49 Retirements from the maintained schools sector: type of award by sex and age on retirement: 2000-01[1]

ENGLAND

	Premature	Actuarially Reduced Benefit	Age	Ill-health	Total
Men					
Under 30	-	-	-	-	-
30-34	-	-	-	-	-
35-39	-	-	-	10	10
40-44	-	-	-	40	40
45-49	-	-	-	230	230
50-54	490	-	-	530	1,020
55-59	620	140	-	210	970
60-64	30	-	840	-	870
65 & over	-	-	50	-	60
all ages	1,140	140	890	1,040	3,200
Women					
Under 30	-	-	-	-	-
30-34	-	-	-	10	10
35-39	-	-	-	30	30
40-44	-	-	-	90	90
45-49	-	-	-	330	330
50-54	590	-	-	680	1,260
55-59	880	420	10	440	1,740
60-64	40	-	2,890	-	2,930
65 & over	-	-	90	-	90
all ages	1,500	420	2,990	1,580	6,480
Men and women					
Under 30	-	-	-	10	10
30-34	-	-	-	10	10
35-39	-	-	-	40	40
40-44	-	-	-	130	130
45-49	-	-	-	560	560
50-54	1,080	-	-	1,210	2,280
55-59	1,500	550	10	650	2,710
60-64	70	-	3,720	-	3,790
65 & over	-	-	150	-	150
all ages	2,640	550	3,880	2,610	9,680

Source: Database of Teacher Records and Pensioner Statistical System (PENSTATS).

1. Data are provisional.

RETIREMENTS

Retirements from the maintained schools sector: type of award and sex by year of retirement, new[1] and current[2] awards and average benefits[3] awarded

ENGLAND

	Premature[4]			Age		
	Men	Women	All	Men	Women	All
1996-97						
New[1] awards						
Number	3,840	6,370	10,210	690	2,590	3,270
Average benefits[3]	£9,800	£7,100	£8,100	£7,100	£4,600	£5,100
Current[2] awards	45,830	72,880	118,710	24,900	64,630	89,530
1997-98						
New[1] awards						
Number	4,400	7,090	11,490	740	2,730	3,480
Average benefits[3]	£9,900	£7,000	£8,100	£8,100	£5,000	£5,700
Current[2] awards	49,600	79,450	129,050	24,210	64,690	88,890
1998-99[5]						
New[1] awards						
Number	970	1,450	2,420	750	2,810	3,560
Average benefits[3]	£7,840	£5,690	£6,550	£8,470	£5,160	£5,860
Current[2] awards	49,950	80,360	130,310	23,530	64,680	88,210
1999-00[5]						
New[1] awards						
Number	1,150	1,530	2,670	870	3,090	3,960
Average benefits[3]	£8,300	£5,980	£6,970	£8,620	£5,540	£6,220
Current[2] awards	50,350	81,220	131,570	22,950	64,990	87,940
2000-01[5]						
New[1] awards						
Number	1,280	1,920	3,190	890	2,990	3,880
Average benefits[3]	£9,950	£6,880	£8,110	£9,870	£6,090	£6,960
Current[2] awards	50,970	82,530	133,500	22,570	65,430	88,010

CONTINUED
RETIREMENTS
Retirements from the maintained schools sector: type of award and sex by year of retirement, new[1] and current[2] awards and average benefits[3] awarded
ENGLAND

	Ill-health			Total		
	Men	Women	All	Men	Women	All
1996-97						
New[1] awards						
Number	1,810	3,170	4,980	6,340	12,120	18,460
Average benefits[3]	£9,700	£7,500	£8,300	£9,500	£6,700	£7,600
Current[2] awards	19,000	35,270	54,270	89,730	172,780	262,510
1997-98						
New[1] awards						
Number	1,210	2,090	3,300	6,360	11,910	18,270
Average benefits[3]	£9,900	£7,800	£8,600	£9,700	£6,700	£7,700
Current[2] awards	19,930	36,950	56,880	93,740	181,090	274,820
1998-99[5]						
New[1] awards						
Number	860	1,460	2,320	2,580	5,720	8,300
Average benefits[3]	£10,360	£7,920	£8,830	£8,860	£6,000	£6,890
Current[2] awards	20,480	37,920	58,400	93,960	182,960	276,920
1999-00[5]						
New[1] awards						
Number	870	1,480	2,350	2,880	6,100	8,980
Average benefits[3]	£10,560	£8,270	£9,110	£9,080	£6,310	£7,200
Current[2] awards	21,030	38,970	60,000	94,340	185,170	279,510
2000-01[5]						
New[1] awards						
Number	1,040	1,580	2,610	3,200	6,480	9,680
Average benefits[3]	£11,780	£8,870	£10,020	£10,520	£7,000	£8,160
Current[2] awards	21,730	40,070	61,790	95,270	188,030	283,300

Source: Database of Teacher Records and Pensioner Statistical System (PENSTATS).

1. 'New' is defined as those awarded retirement benefits in the financial year shown.
2. 'Current' includes teachers awarded retirement benefits in the current financial year plus those awarded benefits in a previous financial year and who are still receiving benefits up to the end of the year shown.
3. This is the average of the annual pension and does not include the one-off 'lump-sum' payments.
4. Premature includes Actuarially Reduced Benefit retirements.
5. Provisional data.

OUT OF SERVICE TEACHERS AGED UNDER 60

Qualified teachers out of service[1,2] at 31 March 2000 aged under 60 who were previously in service, by last known sector, calendar year of last service, sex and age at 31 March 2000[3]

ENGLAND (thousands)

	Nursery and primary					Secondary					Special				
	Calendar year of last service					Calendar year of last service					Calendar year of last service				
	before 1985	1985 to 1989	1990 to 1994	1995 to 2000	all years	before 1985	1985 to 1989	1990 to 1994	1995 to 2000	all years	before 1985	1985 to 1989	1990 to 1994	1995 to 2000	all years
Men															
Under 25	-	-	-	-	-	-	-	-	0.1	0.1	-	-	-	-	-
25-29	-	-	-	0.5	0.5	-	-	-	1.6	1.6	-	-	-	-	-
30-34	-	-	0.2	0.7	0.9	-	0.1	0.7	2.0	2.8	-	-	-	0.1	0.1
35-39	-	0.2	0.3	0.6	1.1	0.2	1.4	1.1	1.5	4.1	-	-	-	0.1	0.2
40-44	0.2	0.2	0.3	0.5	1.1	2.1	2.2	1.0	1.4	6.7	-	0.1	0.1	0.1	0.3
45-49	1.0	0.3	0.4	0.7	2.3	7.3	2.1	1.4	1.9	12.7	0.2	0.1	0.1	0.2	0.5
50-54	2.9	0.4	0.4	0.6	4.2	11.5	1.9	1.4	1.6	16.4	0.2	0.1	0.1	0.1	0.5
55-59	2.2	0.3	0.2	0.1	2.8	9.4	1.0	0.6	0.5	11.5	0.2	-	-	-	0.3
Total	6.3	1.4	1.7	3.6	13.0	30.5	8.6	6.2	10.6	55.9	0.6	0.3	0.3	0.6	1.9
Women															
Under 25	-	-	-	0.3	0.3	-	-	-	0.2	0.2	-	-	-	-	-
25-29	-	-	0.1	4.4	4.5	-	-	0.1	3.4	3.5	-	-	-	0.1	0.1
30-34	-	0.2	2.2	5.9	8.3	-	0.1	1.5	4.3	6.0	-	-	0.1	0.2	0.3
35-39	0.1	1.7	3.2	3.9	8.8	0.2	2.4	2.5	3.6	8.7	-	0.1	0.2	0.3	0.5
40-44	1.8	2.0	2.1	3.0	8.8	3.9	3.5	2.4	3.4	13.1	0.2	0.3	0.2	0.3	1.0
45-49	8.2	2.0	2.5	3.9	16.6	11.4	3.0	2.4	3.9	20.7	0.5	0.2	0.2	0.4	1.3
50-54	15.6	2.0	2.4	3.6	23.5	16.8	2.7	2.5	3.4	25.4	0.8	0.2	0.2	0.3	1.4
55-59	13.1	1.4	1.6	1.5	17.6	16.0	2.0	1.7	1.7	21.4	0.5	0.1	0.1	0.1	0.9
Total	38.7	9.3	14.1	26.3	88.3	48.3	13.7	13.1	23.9	99.0	2.1	0.9	0.9	1.7	5.5
Men and women															
Under 25	-	-	-	0.4	0.4	-	-	-	0.3	0.3	-	-	-	-	-
25-29	-	-	0.1	4.9	5.0	-	-	0.1	5.0	5.1	-	-	-	0.1	0.1
30-34	-	0.2	2.5	6.5	9.2	-	0.2	2.2	6.4	8.8	-	-	0.1	0.3	0.4
35-39	0.1	1.9	3.5	4.4	9.9	0.4	3.8	3.6	5.1	12.8	-	0.1	0.2	0.4	0.7
40-44	2.0	2.2	2.3	3.4	9.9	6.0	5.7	3.4	4.8	19.9	0.2	0.3	0.2	0.4	1.2
45-49	9.2	2.3	2.8	4.6	18.9	18.7	5.1	3.8	5.8	33.4	0.7	0.3	0.3	0.5	1.8
50-54	18.5	2.3	2.8	4.1	27.7	28.3	4.6	3.9	4.9	41.7	1.0	0.3	0.3	0.4	2.0
55-59	15.3	1.7	1.8	1.6	20.4	25.4	3.0	2.3	2.2	32.9	0.8	0.2	0.2	0.2	1.2
Total	45.0	10.7	15.8	29.9	101.4	78.8	22.3	19.3	34.5	154.9	2.7	1.2	1.2	2.3	7.4

OUT OF SERVICE TEACHERS AGED UNDER 60

51a

Qualified teachers out of service[1,2] at 31 March 2000 aged under 60 who were previously in service, by last known sector, calendar year of last service, sex and age at 31 March 2000[3]

ENGLAND
(thousands)

	Other[4]					Total				
	Calendar year of last service					Calendar year of last service				
	before 1985	1985 to 1989	1990 to 1994	1995 to 2000	all years	before 1985	1985 to 1989	1990 to 1994	1995 to 2000	all years
Men										
Under 25	-	-	-	-	-	-	-	-	0.1	0.1
25-29	-	-	-	0.2	0.2	-	-	-	2.3	2.4
30-34	-	-	0.1	0.4	0.5	-	0.1	1.0	3.2	4.2
35-39	-	0.2	0.2	0.4	0.8	0.2	1.8	1.6	2.6	6.1
40-44	0.3	0.4	0.3	0.6	1.6	2.6	2.9	1.7	2.6	9.8
45-49	0.9	0.6	0.6	1.0	3.1	9.4	3.1	2.4	3.7	18.6
50-54	1.6	0.7	0.7	0.9	3.9	16.3	3.1	2.5	3.1	25.0
55-59	1.8	0.5	0.3	0.3	2.9	13.7	1.7	1.2	1.0	17.6
Total	4.7	2.4	2.1	3.8	13.0	42.1	12.7	10.3	18.6	83.8
Women										
Under 25	-	-	-	-	-	-	-	-	0.6	0.6
25-29	-	-	-	0.6	0.6	-	-	0.2	8.5	8.7
30-34	-	-	0.2	1.0	1.2	-	0.3	4.1	11.4	15.7
35-39	-	0.4	0.6	0.9	1.9	0.3	4.6	6.4	8.6	19.9
40-44	0.6	0.8	0.6	1.0	3.0	6.4	6.5	5.2	7.7	25.8
45-49	1.5	0.7	0.6	1.4	4.1	21.6	5.9	5.7	9.5	42.7
50-54	2.2	0.7	0.7	1.4	5.1	35.4	5.5	5.8	8.6	55.4
55-59	2.0	0.5	0.5	0.7	3.7	31.6	4.1	3.9	4.0	43.6
Total	6.3	3.1	3.2	7.0	19.5	95.3	27.0	31.2	58.9	212.4
Men and women										
Under 25	-	-	-	-	-	-	-	-	0.7	0.7
25-29	-	-	-	0.8	0.8	-	-	0.2	10.8	11.0
30-34	-	-	0.3	1.4	1.7	-	0.4	5.0	14.6	20.0
35-39	-	0.6	0.7	1.3	2.7	0.5	6.3	8.0	11.2	26.1
40-44	0.9	1.2	0.9	1.6	4.5	9.0	9.4	6.9	10.3	35.6
45-49	2.4	1.3	1.2	2.3	7.2	31.0	9.0	8.0	13.2	61.3
50-54	3.9	1.4	1.4	2.3	9.0	51.7	8.7	8.3	11.8	80.4
55-59	3.8	1.0	0.8	1.0	6.6	45.3	5.8	5.1	5.0	61.2
Total	10.9	5.5	5.3	10.8	32.5	137.4	39.6	41.6	77.5	296.2

Source: Database of Teacher Records.

1. Excluding those who are receiving a pension from the Teachers Pension Scheme (TPS).
2. Some in service teachers may be shown as not in service because their service details are not recorded. These may include qualified teachers in the 'old' university sector, teachers in the independent sector who are not members of the Teachers Pension Scheme (TPS), part-time teachers outside the maintained nursey, primary and secondary sector who are not members of the TPS.
3. Provisional data.
4. Other includes the independent sector, further and higher education.

51b OUT OF SERVICE TEACHERS AGED UNDER 60

Qualified teachers who have never been in service[1] up to 31 March 2000 aged under 60, by calendar year qualified, sex and age at 31 March 2000[2]

ENGLAND   (thousands)

				Calendar year qualified					
	before 1985	1985 to 1989	1990 to 1994	1995	1996	1997	1998	1999	all years
Men									
Under 25	-	-	-	-	-	0.1	0.3	0.5	0.9
25-29	-	-	0.5	0.5	0.6	0.6	0.6	0.5	3.3
30-34	-	0.4	1.3	0.3	0.3	0.3	0.3	0.3	3.1
35-39	0.6	1.3	0.7	0.2	0.2	0.2	0.2	0.2	3.5
40-44	3.9	0.5	0.4	0.1	0.1	0.1	0.1	0.1	5.3
45-49	5.6	0.2	0.3	0.1	0.1	0.1	0.1	0.1	6.5
50-54	3.5	0.1	0.2	0.1	0.1	-	-	-	4.0
55-59	1.8	0.1	0.1	-	-	-	-	-	2.0
Total	15.4	2.5	3.6	1.2	1.3	1.4	1.5	1.7	28.6
Women									
Under 25	-	-	-	-	-	0.2	0.9	1.8	2.9
25-29	-	-	1.2	1.1	1.4	1.4	1.3	1.2	7.6
30-34	-	0.8	2.6	0.5	0.5	0.4	0.4	0.5	5.7
35-39	1.4	2.2	1.0	0.3	0.3	0.3	0.3	0.4	6.1
40-44	10.7	0.6	0.6	0.2	0.2	0.2	0.3	0.3	13.2
45-49	9.6	0.4	0.5	0.2	0.1	0.1	0.1	0.1	11.2
50-54	4.5	0.3	0.4	0.1	0.1	0.1	0.1	-	5.4
55-59	2.4	0.1	0.1	-	-	-	-	-	2.7
Total	28.6	4.4	6.4	2.3	2.6	2.8	3.3	4.4	54.8
Men and women									
Under 25	-	-	-	-	-	0.3	1.1	2.4	3.8
25-29	-	-	1.7	1.6	2.0	2.1	1.9	1.7	10.9
30-34	-	1.1	4.0	0.8	0.7	0.7	0.7	0.8	8.8
35-39	1.9	3.6	1.8	0.4	0.4	0.5	0.4	0.6	9.6
40-44	14.7	1.1	1.0	0.3	0.3	0.3	0.4	0.4	18.5
45-49	15.2	0.5	0.8	0.3	0.2	0.2	0.2	0.2	17.6
50-54	8.0	0.4	0.6	0.1	0.1	0.1	0.1	0.1	9.4
55-59	4.3	0.2	0.2	-	-	-	-	-	4.8
Total	44.0	6.9	10.0	3.6	3.9	4.2	4.8	6.1	83.4

Source: Database of Teacher Records

1. Some in service teachers may be shown as not in service because their service details are not recorded. These may include qualified teachers in the 'old' university sector, teachers in the independent sector who are not members of the Teachers Pension Scheme (TPS), part-time teachers outside the maintained nursey, primary and secondary sector who are not members of the TPS.
2. Data are provisional.

52

FURTHER EDUCATION
Adult/community/youth centres[1]: 1996 to 2001 by type of centre and type of contract

ENGLAND

	1996	1997	1998	1999	2000	2001
All lecturers	7,040	6,790	6,280	7,020	6,770	5,760
of which:						
Adult or community education centres	6,490	6,230	5,920	6,540	6,260	5,320
Youth clubs and centres	420	390	230	340	340	320
Elsewhere	140	160	130	140	170	120
Full-time	1,260	1,190	1,040	2,000	2,170	1,130
Part-time	5,780	5,600	5,240	5,010	4,600	4,630

Source: DfES annual 618G survey.

1. Lecturers employed by local authorities to provide FE for adults or FE for young people as part of an authorities youth service.

ENGLAND

	Graduates[3]						Graduate status not known	All lecturers		
	Mathematics	Science (including medicine)	Technology	Agriculture	Other subjects	Total		Number	Percentage of total	Cumulative percentage
Men										
Under 25	-	-	-	-	20	30	30	60	0.2	0.2
25-29	40	40	10	-	260	360	300	660	2.6	2.8
30-34	80	120	40	10	610	850	810	1,660	6.6	9.4
35-39	100	220	60	20	930	1,330	1,460	2,790	11.1	20.5
40-44	160	400	150	30	1,430	2,170	2,060	4,230	16.8	37.2
45-49	240	630	230	30	2,130	3,270	2,550	5,820	23.1	60.3
50-54	270	630	310	40	2,320	3,570	3,020	6,580	26.1	86.4
55-59	80	280	90	20	740	1,220	1,470	2,690	10.7	97.0
60 and over	20	50	30	-	210	300	440	740	3.0	100
All ages	990	2,370	920	160	8,640	13,080	12,140	25,220	100	
Women										
Under 25	-	-	-	-	40	50	40	90	0.5	0.5
25-29	30	60	-	10	390	490	490	980	4.9	5.4
30-34	40	90	10	10	640	790	960	1,750	8.7	14.1
35-39	70	130	10	10	860	1,070	1,320	2,390	11.9	26.0
40-44	90	230	30	10	1,320	1,670	1,850	3,520	17.5	43.5
45-49	150	310	20	10	1,850	2,330	2,420	4,750	23.7	67.2
50-54	140	330	20	-	1,680	2,180	2,460	4,640	23.1	90.2
55-59	60	100	-	-	620	780	930	1,710	8.5	98.8
60 and over	-	10	-	-	90	100	150	250	1.2	100
All ages	570	1,270	90	60	7,480	9,470	10,620	20,090	100	
Men and Women										
Under 25	-	10	-	-	60	80	70	150	0.3	0.3
25-29	70	100	20	20	660	850	780	1,640	3.6	3.9
30-34	110	210	50	20	1,240	1,630	1,780	3,410	7.5	11.5
35-39	170	350	70	30	1,790	2,410	2,780	5,190	11.4	22.9
40-44	250	630	170	40	2,750	3,830	3,910	7,740	17.1	40.0
45-49	390	940	250	40	3,980	5,600	4,970	10,570	23.3	63.3
50-54	410	960	330	50	4,000	5,740	5,480	11,220	24.8	88.1
55-59	140	390	100	20	1,360	2,000	2,400	4,400	9.7	97.8
60 and over	20	60	30	-	290	410	590	1,000	2.2	100
All ages	1,560	3,640	1,010	220	16,120	22,550	22,760	45,300	100	

Source: Database of Teacher Records.

1. Provisional data.
2. Including sixth form colleges.
3. Including graduate equivalents.

54

ENGLAND

	Up to £18,999	£19,000 -22,999	£23,000 -26,999	£27,000 -30,999	£31,000 -34,999	£35,000 and over	Salary not known	Total	Average Salary (£)
Men									
Under 25	50	-	-	-	-	-	-	60	16,350
25-29	310	240	50	10	-	-	40	660	19,180
30-34	360	600	440	120	10	10	130	1,660	21,720
35-39	280	640	1,060	410	70	50	290	2,790	24,010
40-44	280	580	1,750	800	210	170	440	4,230	25,700
45-49	210	600	2,420	1,150	410	440	590	5,820	27,250
50-54	160	550	2,580	1,450	480	670	700	6,580	28,340
55-59	70	210	1,060	610	160	320	250	2,690	28,840
60 and over	30	60	310	180	40	70	60	740	28,180
All ages	1,740	3,490	9,670	4,720	1,380	1,720	2,510	25,220	26,500
Women									
Under 25	90	10	-	-	-	-	-	90	16,190
25-29	480	340	80	10	-	-	70	980	19,030
30-34	420	630	420	110	10	-	170	1,750	21,410
35-39	360	580	780	310	60	30	280	2,390	23,410
40-44	320	710	1,310	550	140	100	380	3,520	24,680
45-49	300	690	1,960	790	280	220	520	4,750	25,820
50-54	200	510	1,980	930	280	240	510	4,640	26,510
55-59	60	180	700	350	110	110	210	1,710	26,970
60 and over	10	30	120	60	10	10	20	250	25,970
All ages	2,240	3,660	7,350	3,110	880	710	2,140	20,090	24,810
Men and Women									
Under 25	140	10	-	-	-	-	-	150	16,250
25-29	790	580	130	30	-	-	110	1,640	19,090
30-34	780	1,230	850	230	20	10	300	3,410	21,560
35-39	640	1,220	1,840	720	130	80	570	5,190	23,730
40-44	600	1,290	3,070	1,350	350	270	820	7,740	25,240
45-49	500	1,290	4,380	1,940	680	660	1,110	10,570	26,610
50-54	360	1,060	4,570	2,370	750	910	1,200	11,220	27,590
55-59	130	380	1,760	960	270	430	460	4,400	28,130
60 and over	40	90	430	240	50	70	70	1,000	27,620
All ages	3,970	7,140	17,030	7,830	2,260	2,430	4,650	45,310	25,760

Source: Database of Teacher Records.

1. Including sixth form colleges.

FURTHER EDUCATION
Retirements from further education establishments: type of award by year of retirement, new[1] and current[2] awards and average benefits[3] awarded

ENGLAND

	Premature[4]			Age		
	Men	Women	All	Men	Women	All
1996-97						
New[1] awards						
Number	2,390	1,060	3,450	330	140	470
Average benefits[3]	£8,330	£6,100	£7,640	£6,190	£3,710	£5,440
Current[2] awards	19,900	6,480	26,380	7,630	2,940	10,570
1997-98						
New[1] awards						
Number	2,120	1,220	3,340	330	200	530
Average benefits[3]	£8,700	£6,000	£7,700	£7,500	£3,800	£6,100
Current[2] awards	22,130	7,740	29,870	7,860	4,000	11,860
1998-99[5]						
New[1] awards						
Number	50	20	70	390	240	630
Average benefits[3]	£9,000	£7,100	£8,500	£6,800	£4,400	£5,900
Current[2] awards	23,210	7,920	31,130	8,310	4,180	12,500
1999-00[5]						
New[1] awards						
Number	50	30	80	430	270	700
Average benefits[3]	£10,100	£5,000	£8,400	£7,300	£4,100	£6,000
Current[2] awards	22,900	7,880	30,780	8,400	4,310	12,710
2000-01[5]						
New[1] awards						
Number	120	90	220	430	310	740
Average benefits[3]	£9,080	£5,350	£7,490	£8,390	£4,700	£6,830
Current[2] awards	22,630	7,900	30,540	8,480	4,500	12,970

55

FURTHER EDUCATION

Retirements from further education establishments: type of award by year of retirement, new[1] and current[2] awards and average benefits[3] awarded

ENGLAND

	Ill-health			Total		
	Men	Women	All	Men	Women	All
1996-97						
New[1] awards						
Number	390	280	670	3,100	1,490	4,580
Average benefits[3]	£8,050	£6,680	£7,470	£8,070	£5,980	£7,390
Current[2] awards	3,200	1,770	4,970	30,730	11,180	41,920
1997-98						
New[1] awards						
Number	300	240	540	2,750	1,650	4,400
Average benefits[3]	£8,200	£6,900	£7,600	£8,500	£5,900	£7,500
Current[2] awards	3,470	2,020	5,490	33,460	13,760	47,220
1998-99[5]						
New[1] awards						
Number	180	100	280	610	360	980
Average benefits[3]	£8,000	£5,900	£7,200	£7,300	£5,000	£6,400
Current[2] awards	3,720	2,150	5,870	35,250	14,250	49,500
1999-00[5]						
New[1] awards						
Number	170	130	300	650	430	1,080
Average benefits[3]	£8,800	£6,500	£7,800	£7,900	£4,800	£6,700
Current[2] awards	3,820	2,260	6,090	35,120	14,450	49,570
2000-01[5]						
New[1] awards						
Number	180	150	330	730	550	1,280
Average benefits[3]	£9,530	£7,080	£8,420	£8,780	£5,440	£7,350
Current[2] awards	3,920	2,390	6,310	35,030	14,790	49,820

Source: Database of Teacher Records and Pensioner Statistical System (PENSTATS).

1. 'New' is defined as those awarded retirement benefits in the financial year shown.
2. 'Current' includes teachers awarded retirement benefits in the current financial year plus those awarded benefits in a previous financial year and who are still receiving benefits up to the end of the years shown.
3. This is the average of the annual pension and does not include the one-off 'lump-sum' payments.
4. Premature includes Actuarially Reduced Benefit retirements.
5. Provisional data.

Full-time academic staff in higher education: graduate status and degree subject by sex and age, 31 March 2000[1,2]

ENGLAND

	Graduates[3]						Graduate status not known	All lecturers		
	Mathe-matics	Science (including medicine)	Tech-nology	Agri-culture	Other subjects	Total		Number	Percentage of total	Cumulative percentage
Men										
Under 25	-	-	-	-	-	-	10	10	0.1	0.1
25-29	20	10	10	-	100	150	170	320	2.1	2.1
30-34	40	100	40	10	350	530	570	1,100	7.1	9.3
35-39	60	180	80	10	560	890	890	1,770	11.5	20.8
40-44	90	210	120	-	750	1,170	1,030	2,200	14.3	35.0
45-49	150	300	170	10	1,130	1,760	1,270	3,030	19.7	54.7
50-54	230	380	250	20	1,560	2,430	1,500	3,920	25.5	80.2
55-59	110	300	150	10	770	1,350	900	2,250	14.6	94.8
60 and over	40	120	50	-	290	500	310	800	5.2	100
All ages	750	1,590	880	50	5,500	8,770	6,640	15,410	100	
Women										
Under 25	-	-	-	-	-	-	10	10	0.1	0.1
25-29	10	20	-	-	80	120	150	270	3.2	3.3
30-34	20	60	-	-	320	410	430	840	10.1	13.4
35-39	30	90	20	-	420	560	660	1,220	14.6	28.0
40-44	30	120	10	-	600	760	850	1,610	19.3	47.3
45-49	60	120	10	-	730	920	910	1,830	21.9	69.2
50-54	50	130	10	-	720	910	810	1,720	20.6	89.8
55-59	20	40	-	-	290	350	320	680	8.1	97.9
60 and over	-	10	-	-	70	80	90	170	2.1	100
All ages	210	590	60	20	3,230	4,120	4,240	8,350	100	
Men and Women										
Under 25	-	-	-	-	10	10	10	20	0.1	0.1
25-29	30	40	10	-	190	270	310	580	2.4	2.5
30-34	60	160	40	10	670	940	1,000	1,940	8.2	10.7
35-39	90	270	100	20	970	1,450	1,550	2,990	12.6	23.3
40-44	120	320	130	-	1,350	1,930	1,880	3,810	16.0	39.3
45-49	210	420	190	10	1,860	2,680	2,180	4,860	20.5	59.8
50-54	270	500	270	20	2,280	3,330	2,310	5,650	23.8	83.6
55-59	130	350	150	10	1,070	1,700	1,230	2,930	12.3	95.9
60 and over	40	130	50	-	360	580	400	980	4.1	100
All ages	960	2,180	940	70	8,730	12,890	10,870	23,760	100	

Source: Database of Teacher Records.

1. Provisional data.
2. Not all higher education academic staff are shown because they are not all members of the Teachers Pension Scheme. The total number of full-time academic staff employed by institutions in the higher education sector in England in 1999/00, as recorded by the Higher Education Statistics Agency's Individualised Staff Record, was 113,800.
3. Including graduate equivalents.

HIGHER EDUCATION
Full-time academic staff in higher education: salary ranges by sex and age, 31 March 2000[1,2]

ENGLAND

	Up to £18,999	£19,000 -22,999	£23,000 -26,999	£27,000 -30,999	£31,000 -34,999	£35,000 and over	Salary not known	Total	Average Salary (£)
Men									
Under 25	10	-	-	-	-	-	-	10	17,170
25-29	80	150	60	10	-	-	10	320	20,650
30-34	50	280	430	220	50	20	70	1,100	24,780
35-39	30	160	440	700	240	130	80	1,770	28,570
40-44	20	60	220	950	490	330	120	2,200	31,290
45-49	10	50	170	1,210	610	870	140	3,030	33,430
50-54	10	30	90	1,340	750	1,540	170	3,920	35,340
55-59	-	10	40	730	400	990	90	2,250	36,020
60 and over	-	-	10	280	150	330	30	800	35,670
All ages	190	730	1,460	5,430	2,690	4,200	720	15,410	32,680
Women									
Under 25	10	-	-	-	-	-	-	10	15,530
25-29	70	120	50	10	-	-	10	270	20,790
30-34	40	220	300	180	30	10	60	840	24,640
35-39	20	110	310	520	160	30	70	1,220	27,730
40-44	20	70	220	710	340	170	90	1,610	30,280
45-49	10	50	180	800	410	290	100	1,830	31,560
50-54	10	30	100	700	370	420	100	1,720	32,980
55-59	-	10	30	240	170	200	30	680	34,270
60 and over	-	-	10	50	40	60	10	170	34,840
All ages	190	620	1,200	3,210	1,520	1,170	450	8,350	30,290
Men and Women									
Under 25	20	-	-	-	-	-	-	20	16,350
25-29	150	270	120	20	-	-	30	580	20,710
30-34	90	500	730	400	80	20	130	1,940	24,720
35-39	50	270	750	1,220	400	150	150	2,990	28,230
40-44	40	130	440	1,660	830	500	210	3,810	30,860
45-49	20	100	340	2,010	1,010	1,150	230	4,860	32,730
50-54	20	50	200	2,040	1,120	1,950	270	5,650	34,630
55-59	-	20	70	970	570	1,190	120	2,930	35,620
60 and over	-	-	20	330	200	390	30	980	35,530
All ages	380	1,340	2,660	8,640	4,200	5,360	1,170	23,760	31,840

Source: Database of Teacher Records.

1. Provisional data.
2. Not all higher education academic staff are shown because they are not all members of the Teachers Pension Scheme. The total number of full-time academic staff employed by institutions in the higher education sector in England in 1999/00, as recorded by the Higher Education Statistics Agency's Individualised Staff Record, was 113,800.

58

HIGHER EDUCATION

Retirements from higher education establishments[1]: type of award by year of retirement, new[2] and current[3] awards and average benefits[4] awarded

ENGLAND

	Premature[5]			Age		
	Men	Women	All	Men	Women	All
1996-97						
New[2] awards						
Number	720	170	890	220	60	280
Average benefits[4]	£11,310	£9,220	£10,920	£9,520	£6,520	£8,850
Current[3] awards	7,210	1,480	8,690	2,170	530	2,700
1997-98						
New[2] awards						
Number	1,080	400	1,480	260	60	310
Average benefits[4]	£11,000	£9,000	£10,500	£10,700	£7,100	£10,000
Current[3] awards	7,840	1,780	9,620	2,230	590	2,820
1998-99[6]						
New[2] awards						
Number	100	30	120	240	80	330
Average benefits[4]	£11,200	£9,600	£10,900	£11,000	£7,700	£10,200
Current[3] awards	6,460	1,570	8,030	1,930	580	2,510
1999-00[6]						
New[2] awards						
Number	70	20	90	250	80	330
Average benefits[4]	£12,700	£8,700	£11,700	£10,600	£7,600	£9,900
Current[3] awards	6,460	1,590	8,050	2,120	640	2,760
2000-01[6]						
New[2] awards						
Number	120	40	160	70	40	110
Average benefits[4]	£11,520	£8,830	£10,840	£12,380	£10,010	£11,480
Current[3] awards	6,510	1,610	8,120	2,390	710	3,100

58

HIGHER EDUCATION

Retirements from higher education establishments[1]: type of award by year of retirement, new[2] and current[3] awards and average benefits[4] awarded

ENGLAND

	Ill-health			Total		
	Men	Women	All	Men	Women	All
1996-97						
New[2] awards						
Number	80	60	140	1,020	290	1,300
Average benefits[4]	£10,640	£9,430	£10,130	£10,870	£8,670	£10,390
Current[3] awards	610	270	880	9,990	2,270	12,260
1997-98						
New[2] awards						
Number	80	50	130	1,410	510	1,920
Average benefits[4]	£11,700	£9,200	£10,700	£11,000	£8,800	£10,400
Current[3] awards	650	300	950	10,720	2,670	13,390
1998-99[6]						
New[2] awards						
Number	40	30	70	380	140	520
Average benefits[4]	£10,300	£8,300	£9,500	£11,000	£8,200	£10,200
Current[3] awards	550	280	820	8,940	2,430	11,370
1999-00[6]						
New[2] awards						
Number	50	30	90	370	140	510
Average benefits[4]	£11,300	£9,000	£10,400	£11,100	£8,100	£10,300
Current[3] awards	590	300	900	9,180	2,530	11,710
2000-01[6]						
New[2] awards						
Number	50	30	90	510	170	670
Average benefits[4]	£11,310	£8,990	£10,420	£12,290	£9,470	£11,600
Current[3] awards	650	340	990	9,540	2,660	12,210

Source: Database of Teacher Records and Pensioner Statistical System (PENSTATS).

1. Only retirements from the Teachers Pension Scheme are recorded in this table.
2. 'New' is defined as those awarded retirement benefits in the financial year shown.
3. 'Current' includes teachers awarded retirement benefits in the current financial year plus those awarded benefits in a previous financial year and who are still receiving benefits up to the end of the years shown.
4. This is the average of the annual pension and does not include the one-off 'lump-sum' payments.
5. Premature includes Actuarially Reduced Benefit retirements.
6. Provisional data.